Jack Smith

CATS, DOGS, & OTHER STRANGERS AT MY DOOR

Jack Smith

CATS, DOGS, & OTHER STRANGERS AT MY DOOR

Franklin Watts   1984   *New York   Toronto*

Library of Congress Cataloging in Publication Data

Smith, Jack Clifford, 1916–
Cats, dogs & other strangers at my door.

1. Smith, Jack Clifford, 1916–   —Biography.
2. Pets—California—Anecdotes. 3. Authors, American—
20th century—Biography. I. Title. II. Title: Cats,
dogs, and other strangers at my door.
PS3569.M5375Z464 1984   070'.92'4   84-12008
ISBN 0-531-09751-X

ALSO BY JACK SMITH

How To Win a Pullet Surprise
Jack Smith's L.A.
Spend All Your Kisses, Mr. Smith
The Big Orange
God and Mr. Gomez
Smith on Wry
Three Coins in the Birdbath

AUTHOR'S NOTE

This book could not have been brought into print without the assistance of my wife, Denise Bresson Smith, who not only lived with me and all our animals through all the years it covers, but also worked prodigiously in its preparation and editing, meanwhile working full-time as administrative director of the Southern California Counseling Center.

I am also indebted to my secretary, Marilyn Kelker, for her assiduous research; to my resolute agents, Arthur and Richard Pine; to my charming and fastidious editor, Curtis Kelly; to my gracious publisher, Jon Gillett; and to the publishers and editors of the *Los Angeles Times,* who have sustained me through the years and first published some of the stories that have been adapted for this book.

J.S.

For my family,
including Trevor,
who got left out last time

CATS, DOGS, & OTHER STRANGERS AT MY DOOR

FOREWORD

For more than thirty years Denny and I have lived on Mt. Washington—a low, scrubby old hill near downtown Los Angeles. As the pigeons fly, it is only four miles from City Hall, whose slender white tower is sometimes seen by air travelers on their descent to Los Angeles International Airport.

Before World War I, Mt. Washington enjoyed a decade or two of prosperity and promise. It became a fashionable suburb, with handsome two-story houses in the craftsman style, a serpentine macadam road for motorcars, and an incline railway that climbed directly to a resort hotel at the top.

In the Great Depression, however, it declined. Building stopped. Developments failed. The hotel became a Hindu retreat. The railway went to rust. The upwardly mobile of that era, what few there were, sought each other's company elsewhere. Mt. Washington was then rediscovered by artists, writers, architects, physicians and musicians.

Meanwhile, in canyons thickly overgrown with native scrub, untouched by bulldozers, wildlife thrived: raccoons, opossums, foxes, skunks, rabbits, nonpoisonous snakes, lizards and many species of birds, including the scrub jay, mourning dove, hummingbird, oriole and occasionally a "casual" rarely seen anywhere else in the city.

Thus, thanks to its misfortunes, Mt. Washington was a good place to live in the second half of the twentieth century, if you didn't mind such neighbors, human and otherwise.

Also, we have rarely been without a dog or cat, or both, or more. Most have been strays. Most stayed on. Only a few were deliberately acquired.

Once we brought home a stray mongrel sheepdog that attached herself to us in the streets of another town; we took two flawed poodle pups that a friend couldn't give away; and in mid-life I bought Fleetwood Pugsley, an Airedale, in fulfillment of a boyhood longing. Except for a cockatiel and a canary, he was the only animal we ever purchased.

Our older son, Curt, when he was twelve or so, picked up a stray calico kitten at a motel in Ensenada, Mexico, when we were on vacation there. His brother Doug, when he was a high school boy, brought home a bobtailed kitten someone had left in our car one night.

All the others came to us.

Blackie . . . Chat-Chat . . . Genghis Khan . . . Tweetie . . . Fluff . . . and some that were with us only briefly, and whose names I can't remember.

Neither Denny nor I knew much about pets. My family had taken in a dog or two, but never kept a cat; Denny's family had never owned a dog.

These tales are about dogs and cats, and about birds both wild and caged; and they are about Denny and me, and how we tried to understand these creatures, living unnaturally together with them in an urban world.

It is also the story of my personal rehabilitation: how I have grown and mellowed from a man who distrusted and was baffled by cats, to a man who is still baffled by cats but respects and admires them, and finds them almost as fascinating as women.

1

This all began a long time ago, when Ike was president of the United States and Denny was president of the Mt. Washington Elementary School PTA.

Shaggy was one of those mutts that prove you don't have to have a pedigreed dog to have a dog. She was as doggy looking as a dog could be imagined to look—the kind a cartoonist would draw to show a shaggy dog that obviously was not a particular kind of shaggy dog.

When I took her to the vet the first time, the receptionist asked me what breed she was and I said I didn't know. She looked down over the counter at Shaggy and wrote on the admitting card, "Sheepdog." Probably Shaggy's lineage did go back to the English sheepdog, but not in a very straight line.

She was of medium size, and her coat was turning gray, which led me foolishly to suppose she must be rather an old dog. I didn't really know.

Did dogs turn gray? A grizzled forelock fell down over her eyes so that you never knew whether she was looking at you or not. Part of her upper lip had been chewed off, so that two of her teeth were always bared, and strangers didn't know whether she was sneering or laughing. She had a slight limp, most likely from a brush with a car.

Shaggy was a stray, but she didn't exactly come to our door. One weekend we were visiting Denny's parents up in Bakersfield, in the San Joaquin Valley a hundred miles north of Los Angeles, and Shaggy came to their door. They had never seen her before. It was as if she knew we were in town, and had dropped in to see if we'd take her home with us. Things hadn't gone too well with her in Bakersfield.

To pick up a stray female mongrel a hundred miles from home seemed to me to be taking humanity too far. But she hung around. When the boys came in for dinner, she waited on the front porch. She seemed attached to them already, and she was gentle and patient. No dog is more appealing than a shaggy dog, and of course the boys wanted her.

"If she's still around when we go home," I told them, "you can have her."

I didn't say so, but I wanted to take her home myself. We'd only had one dog, a rather graceful long-haired black dog, with some spaniel or setter or labrador in him, I suspected. The boys, without straining any, had named him Blackie.

Blackie was a handsome dog, with a look of character and breeding, although he had come to us undocumented. He fit easily into the family—a good first dog for all of us, gentle and stable. His only fault was that he loved to run into the street after cars.

Denny and the boys were away one weekend, and the first night, after I had gone to bed, I heard a light impact, and a car braking. Then the car accelerated and sped away and I heard a low, throaty, anguished animal sound, a sort of rattle, growing louder as the animal came closer. I went outside and in the dark I found Blackie dying.

I arranged for the disposal of his body before the family came home, and when they returned on Sunday evening, I told them that Blackie was dead. I was surprised that Denny was the most hurt. The boys seemed to accept it as one of the wonders of life.

"He was the only one that really depended on me," she said.

She was ascribing a self-sufficiency to the boys and me that didn't exist, but I didn't say anything. She had revealed the first sign of an unspoken, undemonstrative affinity for animals that I hadn't suspected, and I don't think she had either.

Shaggy was no bother at all on the drive home over the mountains. We called her Shaggy from the start. I don't remember that there was any discussion— it just seemed inevitable.

She was a good dog.

Or I thought she was.

Until she turned up pregnant.

I was dumbfounded. Because of that forelock

and her grizzled muzzle, I had taken it for granted that she was beyond the breeding age. The father, the boys told me, was a chow that lived down the street. They were more cognizant of such intelligence than I was, and less naive about it.

Shaggy had a litter of eight. One by one I took them to a bar frequented by friends of mine, some of them from the lower walks of life. Whatever hardships life had dealt them, they all had loneliness and gentleness in common. I gave pups to four of them who I thought had the best potential for raising a dog, and found homes for three more of the litter elsewhere. We decided to keep one, a male whose mixed lineage had given him the look of a long-haired golden-red retriever with a white blaze. We called him Blaze.

We learned about dogs from Shaggy and Blaze.

We had no fence then, and it was almost impossible to keep them at home. They were too big for house dogs, and besides their size they had too much outdoor dog in their heritage to be kept indoors.

Denny was always chasing up or down the hill after them when I was away at work. Naturally they followed the boys up the hill to the elementary school. They loved the kids, the games, the snacks from lunchboxes. Denny tried keeping them on leashes but they howled lugubriously, got the chains tangled in the patio furniture, and otherwise harassed her until she would let them loose, hoping they would have forgotten where the school was. They weren't that dumb.

Inevitably, they were caught by the dogcatcher.

Some traitorous teacher at the school saw Blaze and Shaggy on the playground (once too often, evidently) and telephoned the city pound. The subsequent action was swifter, I suspect, than if she had reported an armed robbery. Shaggy and Blaze were picked up and taken in.

That first time, Denny drove to the pound and bailed them out. When it happened a second time, though, she had to go to police court, an experience that was to have a curious epilogue years later.

Shaggy and Blaze weren't bright. If anything, Blaze was even less so than his mother. But he was gentle and charming, and if not ferocious, he was a good barker—that is, he had a good voice, though he was indiscriminating in the objects that provoked its use.

Shaggy was affectionate to a fault. If you rejected her she would simply sit and stare at you— or turn her head your way. You weren't ever sure whether she was actually looking at you, because of the hair in her eyes. Finally you had to relent. She knew it at once, and would limp over and lay her muzzle in your hand, exposed teeth gleaming incongruously in their permanent snarl.

She seemed to like baseball. That is, when the children played baseball in the street she was always there, and they said she was sometimes second base. She didn't *play* second base; she *was* second base. They didn't really have any bag, but Shaggy liked to sit or lie about where second base ought to be, and they counted her as the bag. She got to lick the hand of everyone who made it to second, and she loved it.

2

I didn't even know we had a cat until I saw it one day on the roof of the house next door. I had awakened early, as was my custom, and gone out to get the paper, and was attracted to a commotion on the roof of the Kling house next door.

Three young cats, hardly larger than kittens, were chasing each other about on the shingles, having a good time. One was gray, one appeared to be a Siamese, and the third was what I would have called a pinto (being more familiar with horses), but which I soon found out was called a calico.

I watched the cats on the roof for a minute, admiring their grace and agility, then went back in the house. They were no concern of mine.

As I turned through the paper, though, scanning the news, I kept wondering about them. Whose cats were they? Why hadn't I seen them before?

Our younger son Doug was then at the age where he knew everything that was going on in the neighborhood, except perhaps adultery, whose symptoms he might not yet recognize. I went into his bedroom and shook him by a knee.

"Wake up, sport," I said. "There are three cats on Victoria's roof."

Victoria was the Klings' daughter, a classmate of Doug's.

"That figures," he said. "What color are they?"

I told him one was gray and one was a pinto and one was a Siamese.

"Yep," he said. "That's the ones it would be."

"You know who they are?"

"Was one of them orange and black and white?"

I told him yes, that's what I meant by pinto.

"That one's ours," he said.

"I didn't know we had a cat," I said.

"Pa," he said, "there are a lot of things going on around here that you don't know about."

"All right," I said, "I'm trying to learn. Now what do we do about those cats up on Victoria's roof?"

"We wait until they get hungry, and start to meow. Then we get the ladder and go up on the roof and get them down."

"Did we get a ladder and put the cats up on the roof?" I asked.

"No, they got up there by themselves."

"Then why can't they get down by themselves?" It seemed a reasonable question.

"Because they're cats."

I wondered if he could explain that.

"Cats can get places," he said, "that they can't get down from."

It was a dead end. I might as well change the subject.

"What ever became of your horned toad?" I asked him. "Does he get up on the roof?"

"Horned toads are different than cats."

"Different from," I said. I wanted him to know there were some things I knew.

"They can't get on roofs," he said.

"Then where is he?" I was certainly not afraid of horned toads, but if there was one in the house, I wanted to know where it was.

"He's hibernating."

"Where is he hibernating at?"

"Shouldn't you just say 'Where is he hibernating?' without the 'at'?"

Live by the sword, die by the sword.

"Correct," I said. "Where is he hibernating?"

"That's what we have to find out."

"You mean you think he's somewhere in this house but you don't know exactly where?"

"I'm positive."

"You're positive what?"

"I'm positive I don't know where he is."

"But you think he's in the house?"

"Positive."

"Well, what are we going to do about him?"

"Let him hibernate," he said. "It's their nature, Pa."

"What are we going to do about the cats?"

"Wait until they meow."

"Has our cat got a name?"

He said what sounded like Sha-Sha or Zsa-Zsa.

"It's spelled c-h-a-t," he said. "It's French for cat."

A French name. No doubt Denny had named her, being of French descent. That meant she was in on it. I was outnumbered.

Chat-Chat and I got acquainted one weekend when Denny and the boys went out of town to visit her family.

I knew very little about cats except what I had learned from reading. I had been especially influenced by Kipling's story, "The Cat Who Walked His Wild Lone," which I had read as a child, and I was prepared to find that a cat was more independent than a dog. I have since learned many things about cats, but that one belief about their nature remains intact, abundantly fortified by observation.

I had read somewhere that if you pet a cat one billion times on a cold day, you will generate enough electricity to light a seventy-five-watt bulb for one minute. It did not seem a piece of information that was likely to help either of us through our first trial.

From the cat lore I knew, I was of the opinion that cats had intruded on the human scene, warming themselves at our fires, sipping the milk off our tables, and generally sponging off our hard-won gleanings. They had done little in return but generate electricity—and only a minuscule amount, even if you petted them a billion times.

I was even doubtful that the cat had actually

been worth its keep as a mouser. I had watched cats stalking mice, and observed that often they were merely terrorizing their victims simply for the sport of it. We had all been conditioned by animated comics, and were likely to be more sympathetic toward Mickey Mouse than toward Sylvester the Cat, though I always admired Sylvester for his wit and fortitude.

I did not know then that in the Middle Ages cats did what doctors couldn't do and perhaps kept civilization from perishing altogether in the Great Plague by killing hundreds of thousands of plague-bearing rats. I didn't know that despite this great service to mankind at a moment when it was in mortal peril, the cat was cruelly persecuted for the next four hundred years as an agent of paganism and witchcraft. Even as late as Tudor times cats were burned in public as symbols of heresy, and it was regarded as darkly significant that not once were cats mentioned in the Bible.

I see the cat in a new light, now that I know it was a victim and a survivor of man's inhumanity. I do not care to be among its persecutors.

At the time, however, my attitude toward cats was somewhat in tune with that of the Count de Buffon, the leading naturalist of his time, which happened to be the eighteenth century. The cat, Buffon observed, "possesses an innate malice, and perverse disposition, which increase as they grow up. [It] easily assumes the habits of society, but never acquires its manners. [It] appears to have no feelings which are not interested, to have no affection that is not conditional, and to carry on no intercourse with men, but with a view to turning it to his own advantage. . . . Of all the domestic animals, the character of the cat is the most equivocal and suspicious. He is kept, not for any amiable qualities, but purely with a view to banish rats, mice, and other noxious animals. . . ."

It was with that eighteenth century mind-set, then, despite Buffon's difficulty with pronouns, that I began my life with Chat-Chat and her successors.

At about that time the city attorney of Los Angeles had solemnly advised the Animal Regulation Department that it could not issue permits for the trapping of cats. Residents wanted to trap cats that were trespassing in their yards, and take them to the city pound for disposal.

The city attorney did not say it was against the law to trap a cat. He merely said the law did not clearly say it was all right to trap a cat. This being the case, he advised the Animal Regulation people, they would do well not to issue permits for the trapping of cats.

The language was admirably succinct:

Question: "May the Board of Animal Regulation authorize the trapping of cats within the City of Los Angeles?"

Answer: "No."

He added that cats need not be licensed or leashed. I had always wondered why that was. Why, if cats went free, did I have to buy a license for my big, harmless shaggy dog? It was a misdemeanor for her even to walk half a block down the street to call on a sick friend. She was constantly in peril of being picked up and impounded, and if we failed to bail her out—worse!

It seemed plainly unconstitutional, but dogs were incompetent, of course, to take the matter to court, and this was before the start of the civil rights movement.

What was the principle behind this seeming injustice? Why was my dog restrained and my cat free to explore the hill, peeping, foraging and trespassing, free to walk her wild, lone way, while no man dared set a trap or lay a hand on her?

Of course Governor Adlai Stevenson had enunciated this principle and emancipated cats in Illinois with his famous veto, perhaps the most gracefully written state paper of the century, thereby not only securing the liberty of cats but also enhancing the quality of state prose. Rejecting a bill to require the licensing and restraining of cats, the governor wrote, in part:

"I cannot believe that there is a widespread public demand for this law or that it could, as a practical matter, be enforced.

"Furthermore, I cannot agree that it should be the declared public policy of Illinois that a cat visiting a neighbor's yard or crossing the highway is a public nuisance. It is in the nature of cats to do a certain amount of unescorted roaming. Many live with their owners in apartments or other restricted premises, and I doubt if we want to make their every brief foray an opportunity for a small game hunt by zealous citizens—with traps or otherwise.

"I am afraid this bill could only create discord,

recrimination and enmity. . . . Moreover, cats perform useful service, particularly in rural areas, in combatting rodents—work they necessarily perform alone and without regard for property lines.

"We are all interested in protecting certain varieties of birds. That cats destroy some birds I well know, but I believe this legislation would further but little the worthy cause to which its proponents give such unselfish effort. The problem of cat versus bird is as old as time. If we attempt to resolve it by legislation, who knows but what we may be called upon to take sides as well in the age-old problems of dog versus cat, bird versus bird, or even bird versus worm.

"For these reasons, and not because I love birds the less or cats the more, I veto and withhold my approval from Senate Bill No. 93. . . ."

Of all the political pronouncements that came down to us in the postwar era, I believe that veto by Adlai Stevenson had the most profound effect on my thinking, and did the most to change my ways.

To think that we might have had that man for president!

Chat-Chat and I got along quite well that weekend, though I didn't know how to talk to her. She jumped up on the couch and into my lap when she wanted either companionship or dinner, and not knowing which, I gave her both.

It was the beginning of a long and sometimes difficult period of enlightenment in my life, one rather late in coming, but one which, in the end, I was to enjoy.

3

Gato was Mexican, which is why we named her Gato, the Spanish word for cat.

She was a calico of good color and good character, that is to say, she was just what a cat should be. And she was to be our cat so many years that I don't really know how old she was when we saw her for the last time—at least thirteen, we think.

She gave us one litter of kittens, a calamity for which, of course, I must take all but the biological responsibility. That belonged to a monstrous tomcat that preyed on virgins in our block for years, evidently escaping retribution by falling back on all nine of his lives.

We had picked up Gato at a cheap motel in Ensenada, sixty miles south of Tijuana. She had strolled into the boys' cottage, still wobbly, and Curt had taken her in. She was a pretty kitten, and I like calicos. She looked too little to have been weaned, but she seemed to have been cast out. She was alone and lonely.

She was infested with Mexican fleas, which may be no larger than American fleas, but which on her looked as big as Egyptian beetles. We got rid of them by washing her in vodka, which is duty-free and cheap in Mexico. The fleas died in their tracks, like bulls in the Tijuana bull-ring.

I didn't know whether we would need some kind of papers to get her across the border. We try to be good citizens. I phoned the Mexican Tourist Bureau. They told us the cat must be vaccinated. We found a veterinarian who told us the cat was too little to be vaccinated. He directed us to the Edificio Municipale. They would issue the necessary papers. Having no Spanish, we blundered our way through a labyrinth of bureaus and finally stood before a solemn little man who regarded us with suspicion from his swivel chair— the embodiment of petty authority.

I tried to explain, pointing to Doug, who was holding the kitten, and saying we wanted to take it to the United States, and we wanted to know did we need any papers.

"He was born in Mexico?" the man said, groping for the English words.

"Yes," I said, relieved that he spoke English at all.

"His name?" he asked.

"His name," I said, "is Gato."

For a moment the man looked incredulous, raising his eyebrows. Then comprehension dawned. He collapsed in laughter.

"El gato!" he shrieked. "I thought you mean el muchacho! The boy!"

Mexico, he explained, when he had recovered, did not care whether we took the cat out or not. It was up to the American customs officers at the border.

When we reached the border we simply didn't declare our passenger, and either the customs officer didn't notice her, or decided to overlook it.

That is how Gato became an illegal American.

She was a clean cat. The Mexican vodka seemed to have done the job. We never noticed fleas on her again, and a good thing, too. In the United States we couldn't afford to wash our cats in vodka.

It was Doug who broke the news to me one day that she was pregnant.

"How do you know?" I asked.

He shrugged. "You can tell."

He was in high school by that time and had shown more of a flair for science and biology than I ever had. I decided to accept his diagnosis, as disagreeable as it was.

"How long does it take?" I asked.

"You mean what's the gestation period?"

"Yes, I guess that's what I mean."

"I'll look it up," he said, and headed for the encyclopedia. It was what I had taught them both to do, by my example, whenever a question of fact came up.

He found it: "The gestation period for cats," he read, "is fifty-five to sixty-three days."

If he was right about Gato, that didn't give me much time. I had to find homes for the kittens. I couldn't take them down to the Continental Bar & Grill and pass them off on the habitués, either, the way I had with some of Shaggy's pups. Kittens weren't as easy to pass off. Besides, I didn't dare try to work that ground again.

She had a litter of five. Unfortunately, the kittens did not resemble their mother. Their father's genes prevailed. They were a motley and undistinguished lot, but like all kittens, irresistible.

By the time they were weaned I had lined up homes for all, and hand-delivered them myself, though it took a day and many miles of driving. I placed them in better neighborhoods than the one they left, and for all I know, they may be alive and happy to this day.

Chat-Chat was still with us when Gato joined our ménage. They didn't become pals, the way dogs do; cats don't form quick and lasting alliances with other cats. But they shared the territory with mutual forbearance and respect.

Chat-Chat's tenure was not long. She soon went the way of cats on our hill—she simply vanished; and Gato moved into a reign that was to be undisputed for years, though, like the medieval barons, she was endlessly challenged by upstarts, brigands, trespassers and poachers of every stripe. But from prurient tomcats she was secure. After that one disaster, I had removed her from the sexual carousel.

She was a good cat, which means that she was clean, quiet, predatory, independent, stubborn, courageous, beautiful and miraculously agile. It was fascinating simply to watch her move—to stretch, walk, spring, sprint, and make incredible, scrambling leaps. Surely the cat is the most supremely gifted of athletes, and the most superbly equipped of hunters.

Watch closely. She strolls in that long, slow, graceful stride. Suddenly she stops, tense, ears up. She has heard or seen her prey. She runs a few steps, stops, lowers herself, belly close to the ground, ears pointed forward, pupils wide; she begins to quiver, her head sways slightly from side to side—to gain a stereoscopic perspective on her target? To triangulate the distance? She lunges, front paws out, claws unleashed. The attack is so swift that the victim is caught before its alarms go off. With a dispatch no matador could match, she sinks her sword teeth into the creature's spine, at the base of the skull, and it is dead.

Where did she learn this routine? Not from her mother; Gato had a mother too short a time. It was in her genes. It came to her directly from the jungle through the bloodline of her ancestor *Felis libyca*, the African wild cat. Centuries of breeding for gentleness and domesticity had altered it not at all—fortunately for the cat, if not for mice and birds.

It took me years to learn this. In the urban patch of jungle that was our backyard, my sympathies and prejudices for a long time were with the birds, and even the lizards, though I coldly consigned our rodents to the cats, and like a gladiator master drove the cats to make more kills.

I was still in that state of naive righteousness the first time I saw a cat catch a bird. It wasn't one of our cats, which made it easier for me. It was one of the neighborhood tomcats, a rogue that trespassed every day, and was always up to no good. By now our cats had been immunized against his lust, at least.

I happened to be in my favorite place, the swivel rocker by the large window that overlooks our backyard, the birdbath, and the rustic canyon below. I have always put out feeders, and, the hill being a natural refuge in the heart of the city, we had an almost constant stream of visitors flying in, like an airport.

The tomcat was crouching among my wife's ranunculuses below the birdbath. A small bird with a pale yellow breast fluttered down from the pine tree and splashed into the birdbath. It might have been a warbler. I began to anthropomorphize him at once. He seemed to be getting a kick out of life. It was a nice morning, a Sunday, as I remember. The bird was flapping his wings in the water and trilling something light (a cadenza from *La Traviata?*) and washing his kneecaps.

Then the cat struck. I realized too late that I should have chased him off. I could at least prevent murder from being done while I was watching. It was my property. The cat leaped over the bowl of the birdbath in a perfect arc, neatly catching the bird in his mouth at the apex of his flight, and landed lightly, on his feet, of course, among the flowers. It was as clean and breathtaking as any trapeze act. Then the cat loped off with his prize.

The back door opened and one of the boys raced through the house toward his bedroom. He had witnessed the kill. In a minute he came out with his bow and arrow.

"What are you going to do?" I asked him.

"I'm going to shoot that cat," he said, as cool as Errol Flynn. "You see him get that bird?"

"No use shooting the cat," I said.

"Pa," he said, "that's a bad cat. He kills our birds and fights our cats."

I tried to explain that it was the nature of cats to hunt birds, and it was the fate of birds to be caught and eaten now and then. That was life in the jungle. Nature in the raw was seldom mild. That's the way it was and it was not man's prerogative to interfere.

I didn't know whether I believed myself entirely; but I knew I didn't want my son shooting a neighbor cat with an arrow.

He saw my point. In fact I think he understood it better than I did. After all, he had known Gato was pregnant before I did. It was just that he had a new bow and arrow, and he had seen this as a chance to use it, like Robin Hood, in a good cause.

4

In our memories we tend to relate small events to larger events that occurred at the same time. Everyone remembers what he or she was doing when the news came that President Kennedy had been shot.

We happened to be watching the 1964 Republican convention on television the night Genghis Khan came into our lives. As things turned out, Genghis Khan was more memorable than the convention.

"What's that?" Denny said suddenly that evening.

She had heard something outside in the night. I believe women have a better ear for intrusive sounds than men. Perhaps it goes back to the cave, when the men were out hunting and the women were guarding the hearth, and fearful of every sound.

"What's what?" I said, hoping it was only a fancy.

"I heard a sound," she said.

"That was Rockefeller growling," I said, thinking levity might drive it away, whatever it was.

"Outside," she said. "It sounded like a kitten. I think it's caught or something."

"It's probably all right," I said. "Cats are always crying in the night."

The convention was getting raucous, and she didn't hear the sound again.

The next night I heard it myself. I knew it wasn't merely a prurient tomcat, calling to its mate. We went outside and listened. It was an anguished meow; a cry for help.

"It's a kitten," Denny said. "It's hurt or hungry."

Curt went into his room and got his flashlight and descended into the canyon, searching through the brush below the road. It seemed five minutes before the animal cries grew suddenly louder and more frantic, and Curt shouted up to us, "I've got it!"

He came crashing back through the brush and into the floodlighted patio with something alive in one arm. It was a yellow cat—still a kitten. It had enormous wild eyes; its coat was unkempt and matted with mud. It snarled and cried.

He took it inside and put it on the carpet. Its crying was incessant. Its tail drooped; its right hind leg dragged. It saw our cat and hissed. Everything was its enemy. Somehow it looked Mongolian, with its wild eyes and ferocious whiskers. I thought of Genghis Khan.

They fed it in the kitchen. It slurped up a bowl

of milk and wolfed a bowl of cat food, too starved to worry about the giants who had it in their power.

"Wretched thing," I said. "We can't just turn it out. You'll have to take it to the pound tomorrow. Have them put it out of its misery."

I knew it was important to plant that idea in my wife's mind before she developed a sentimental feeling for this latest of our foundlings. Charity might begin at home, but it had to end there, too.

"I guess you're right," she said.

The next day when I came home from work I didn't see the yellow cat around.

"You have it taken care of?" I asked.

"Yes. I took it to Dr. Morehouse."

"Dr. Morehouse?"

Morehouse was our veterinarian. He would certainly charge more than the pound to put the cat to sleep. But evidently she felt better about having him do it.

"He took care of it?" I said.

"Yes. He said it was in very poor shape. He said it had a broken leg and a broken tail. It must have been hit by a car."

"What did he charge?" I asked. We'd never asked him to put an animal to sleep for us before.

"He'll bill us afterward," she said. "He has to wait until the cast is off."

"The cast?"

"Yes. He put a cast on its leg and cropped its tail. He said the tail would never work properly. It would just be a drag. He says the poor thing should be as good as new, except for a limp and his short tail."

"His tail?"

"Yes. It's a male, by the way."

"In that case," I said, "we'll call him Genghis Khan."

We quickly shortened his name to Gus. It seemed to suit him—not that Genghis Khan didn't.

With misgiving, I watched Gus grow from a frail kitten with a plaintive voice and great anguished eyes into a ferocious predator with a taste for blood sports and a howl that plucked my spine like an A-string. When he was old enough, naturally, I had him altered, not only to protect the neighborhood females from his sexual aggressions, but also in the hope of tempering somewhat his macho character.

At the time, I saw him as the embodiment of all that I found intimidating and antagonistic in cats; but I see now that there was something admirable about Gus—his independence, his fortitude, his lust for life, and, yes, perhaps there was something lovable about him. At least my wife saw it, and he soon became her favorite.

Once his cast was shed, Gus became a terror in the backyard, amazingly agile despite his limp. He plundered the lizard runs and drove the mockingbirds from the birdbath.

I soon began to think more kindly of Gato, and was sorry that I had once considered her wanton and a barbarian. Compared with Genghis Khan, she was an angel. In time he even turned on her, harassing her from ambush, hijacking her food, usurping her pillow, torturing her sleep.

She fell ill. She turned apathetic, almost as

if in a trance. Her legs seemed paralyzed. She stared without recognition out of unblinking eyes. Alarmed, I took her to the vet's.

Three days later Dr. Morehouse asked me to come and get her. "I can't find anything physically wrong with her, Jack," he said. "She seems to have got over it, whatever it was." Gato looked alert and glad to see me. She wanted to go home.

I told Dr. Morehouse about Gus, and wondered whether he could be making her neurotic.

"That could be," he said. "She acted as if she'd had a crack-up of some kind."

As I recall, cat psychiatry turned out to be no cheaper than cat orthopedics and surgery had been.

After that, we kept Gato indoors most of the time, and she seemed to recover her balance and serenity.

Gus was the wildest cat we ever took in, but I thought he might also be the most intelligent, and I decided to see if we could train him to come to the front door instead of the back door. We had screened in our patio, thus enclosing the back door, and to enter the house it was necessary first to use the new screen door, which was covered with a plastic weatherpane.

Gus had always used the back door, scratching at it when he wanted in, and tough as that door was, it bore his mark. I was afraid he would lacerate the plastic cover of the screen door, not to mention my nerves.

"We have to train him to come round to the front door when he wants in," I told my wife.

"How do we do that?" she asked.

"Condition his reflexes," I said.

She looked skeptical.

"Yes. Like Pavlov. You remember Pavlov's experiments."

"Didn't he work with dogs?"

"Dogs, cats—all the same. It's a matter of association. When you set a plate of food in front of a hungry dog, what does he do?"

"He gulps it down, I imagine."

"Yes. But first he slavers. Right? Pavlov found out that if you ring a bell every time you give a dog a plate of food, pretty soon his tongue will slaver whenever you ring the bell, even if you don't put out any food."

"What's that got to do with getting Gus to come to the front door?"

"Simple. We get a little brass bell. We can use the one you bought me to ring when I was sick. Every time you want to let Gus in, open the front door and ring the bell. When he comes in, feed him. Instantly."

Meanwhile, I cautioned, he was never to be let in by the patio door. "He has to forget that the patio has a door. Don't even use it yourself if you think he's looking."

She found the little bell and followed my instructions. The first day she opened the front door and rang the bell on four or five occasions. Gus did not come. The next day she saw him on the front porch. She opened the door and rang the bell. Gus walked in, waddling from side to side with his usual arrogance.

"Now feed him," I said. "Instantly."

She gave him a bowl she had already prepared.

In the next few days he responded to the bell several times, coming to the front door to get his bowl. Not once did he scratch at the patio door.

"You see?" I said. "It works. Pavlov was right."

One morning a week or so later I happened to look out the window into the backyard. I saw Gus in a motionless crouch, about to pounce on a lizard. I hurried through the house and out the patio door, shouting "No!"

Gus gave up the hunt, streaked past my legs and bounded through the patio door. I leaped for it as it swung shut behind him. I grabbed the handle and yanked, but the door held fast. The automatic latch had done its job.

Genghis Khan had locked me out.

He was with us too short a time. He was an aggressive, wandering cat, and he was not cute. Someone evidently didn't like him. We heard him crying on the porch one morning and found him mortally wounded.

He had been shot in the hind quarter, apparently with a pellet gun. The impact had been enough to tear the flesh severely, but not to kill him outright. He was in shock.

Denny took him down to the hospital and Dr. Morehouse saw him at once. It was no use. Gus was done for.

Denny came home alone. She wept. She had liked Gus best of all.

5

Beau and Jolie were the first pedigreed dogs in our family. Blackie and Shaggy had been strays, and Blaze the offspring of a stray. Whatever their lineage, they turned out to be as good as we deserved.

Blaze, although he had been unwanted and hadn't seemed too promising a pup, came to be loved and useful as a companion and watchdog for a young woman, recently divorced, who lived a block down the street from us with her infant daughter. We found out that Blaze was visiting her and the little girl. They loved him, and it was mutual. When she asked if she could have him, we were pleased. A few months later mother and child moved away, and they took Blaze with them.

Shaggy lived out her years with us—amiable and uncomplaining to the end. We didn't know how old she was, of course, but Denny wasn't very surprised the morning she found Shaggy lying in the leafy walk of the arbor along the north side of the house. She showed no signs of injury, though she may have been hit by a car. On the other hand, she may simply have chosen that soft and shady place to die. We had long since forgiven her those early vagrancies, and also her one great indiscretion. We missed her for a while, but soon Beau and his sister came into our lives.

I always had the idea that pedigreed dogs didn't need people like us. They would find homes. But a friend of Denny's had a registered miniature black poodle that had thrown a litter and evidently she was having trouble disposing of them.

"She wants to give us one," Denny said.

I wasn't thrilled. I knew poodles were superb animals. They were hardy, handsome and intelligent, and had been bred as working dogs. It wasn't their fault that in the United States they had fallen into a life of ease as indoor pets and show dogs. I unfairly associated poodles with the boudoir and satin pillows and perfumed baths. And anyway, if I'd wanted a pedigreed dog I'd have bought an Airedale.

As it turned out, we came home with two poodles. The second one was my idea. They were the last two left in the litter, and I didn't want to separate them.

Both of them were flawed. The female was a runt. She looked more like a toy than a miniature. The male's upper-left canine tooth had grown out so that his lip couldn't close over it. Consequently, the lip was pushed out and up in a permanent sneer. It robbed him of some of the poodle's natural charm, but perhaps it appealed to some maternal instinct in my wife.

It was not hard to see why Denny's friend was giving them away. Neither had a chance as a show dog, and for the good of the breed they would have to be neutered as soon as possible. They wouldn't have brought her much of a price.

Deciding which one to take was a Hobson's choice. It was too early to judge their intelligence. I had an idea they had been rejected by the other pups in the litter, and were already dependent on each other.

"If we're going to take one," I said, "we might as well take them both."

We took them home in a cardboard carton and Denny named them Beau and Jolie, names which, while French enough, seemed comically inappropriate. Beau was well-shaped and jaunty, as a poodle is supposed to be, but you either laughed or shuddered when you saw that sneer. Jolie was not only a runt, but spindly and awkward, like a new lamb. Fortunately, they soon were devoted to each other.

And soon enough they were devoted to Denny.

It was uncanny. They were as attached to her as if they had been bonded to her at birth, like Konrad Lorenz's duck, and she was their surrogate mother. I couldn't see what she did to inspire this adulation.

I did not consider them my personal dogs, though I shared the responsibility for their welfare, including their visits to the vet. I never mis-treated them, except to mutter some mild curse when they frustrated me. Maybe they understood the tone, if not the words. I felt rather like their servant.

Poodles were bred into aristocracy, and it might be that they were ill at ease in the middle-class environment into which we had thrust them. Did they consider me below them?

I was baffled. Dogs have always liked me—even strange ones. I make friends with them instantly. What was it then, between me and the poodles?

They were literally mad about Denny. When she came home they would go into frenzies of exultation, leaping and dashing about and barking until they were quite exhausted; then they would sit at her knee, panting and fawning up at her.

If she went out the front door they would run into my den and jump up on the back of the couch and look out the window, watching her departure. If she walked into another room and shut the door behind her they waited at the door.

I kidded her that I might consult the Hollywood dog psychologist who treated dogs and their owners together. Actors were always coming to him with dogs they thought were neurotic. Usually, of course, the dogs were OK but the actors were neurotic. I didn't really care to pay an exorbitant fee to sit on a couch with my wife's poodles, only to find out I was neurotic. But I did think that a dog that didn't love me must have a personality disorder of some kind.

"It's just your imagination," Denny suggested.

One day the two dogs got out the front door and I went after them. As if by plan, one ran one way, one the other. Since they were almost always inseparable, it looked as if they had split just to confound me. Finally I caught Beau and shut him in the house while I went after Jolie. With Beau out of the game, Jolie gave up and came to me. Once I had them both inside I decided to talk to them as friends, instead of reprimanding them for running out. I knew they wouldn't know what I was reprimanding them for, anyway. If you're going to try to teach an animal by punishment, it has to be instant. You have to catch it in the act. And I don't think even that works. Animal people say the only way to teach an animal to do anything is by reward, and I suspect it's true. It seems to me now that Denny knew this instinctively, all along.

Then one night it finally came to me why the poodles adored her and avoided me.

"I fed the dogs," she said, "would you mind putting them out?"

I felt a lightning bolt of comprehension.

"Would you say that again?"

"I said I fed the dogs, would you mind putting them out? Why?"

So that was it. That had been our ritual night after night, ever since we brought the poodles home.

"You always feed them, don't you?" I said.

"I guess so. Most of the time. Why?"

It took a while, but some changes in routine

were made, and in time the poodles began to like me. But I wouldn't call it love.

I was amused one morning when I found in the mail an invitation from the Kennel Club of Beverly Hills to enter Beau and Jolie in the annual All Breed Dog Show and Obedience Trials, which was said to be the biggest dog show in the world. Maybe I'd do it, just for the chutzpah of it. How amusing it would be to enter that pair and stand beside them, watching the faces of the other fanciers as they contemplated the two poodles—a runt female and a male that looked like Lon Chaney in *The Phantom of the Opera.*

It occurred to me that Beau might be helped by orthodontics. The next time I took him to the vet's to get clipped I asked Tinker Belle, Dr. Morehouse's assistant, about the tooth. (I never knew her name. I called her Tinker Belle because she was so petite and exquisite and had lovely lavender eyes.) She held the poor fellow at arms' length, then clutched him to her bosom, his head against her cheek.

"It's just a little fault," she said, her eyes reproaching me. "He can't help it."

"Can't anything be done?"

"The doctor could pull the tooth," she said, "if it's that important. Or you might try an orthodontist."

Was there a note of scorn in that suggestion? Anyway, I had an idea that a dog orthodontist would cost more than a dog psychologist.

So I didn't enter them in the All Breed show after all, and before the next one came around they had been rendered ineligible by surgery. If there was one thing I didn't want going on in our backyard, it was incest.

6

I first realized we had a new cat in the house on a stormy Thanksgiving Day. For an hour or so in the morning the world had seemed a blameless place, full of simple pleasures.

The storm had let up. We drew back all the curtains. The sun came in. The air was fresh and electric, like sea air after a squall. Gray clouds, shining at their torn edges, parted like an opera set and the sky appeared, pale but well.

"I'm going to make a pumpkin pie," my wife announced. She went into the kitchen and cranked out the casement windows. The whole house took a deep fresh breath.

I stepped down into the patio (which at that time was screened in under an aluminum roof) and removed the plastic storm panels. Outdoors the trees and the flowers were dripping dry. Rainwater shone like mirrors in the birdbath and the barbecue. I propped open a screen door and swept a multitude of torpid insects back into the grass. I emptied the wheelbarrow and the barbecue of rainwater, then went round to the front and brought the paper in.

I put a Mozart serenade for wind instruments on the phonograph. The morning seemed exactly right for the quick pulse of Mozart and the woody sounds of oboe, clarinet and basset horn. I sat at my desk, looking out into the bright street, as the unseen musicians in the living room huffed away at their work for my explicit pleasure.

The scent of baking pumpkin pie floated into the den on an exquisite cadenza. It was redolent of Thanksgivings past, the ripe pumpkin smell of fruition and prosperity.

For a while my life seemed in perfect balance, a masterpiece of harmony. I was at peace. My eye fell warmly on the cat. It had sprung silently to the couch beside the desk and was curled on the pillow. It was very dark brown, almost black, like a mink. Suddenly, it occurred to me that I had never seen that cat before.

"Well," I said, loud enough to get the attention of the household, "Where did this one come from?"

"You mean the kitten?" Denny said. "Doug found it in the car last night after the meeting at the church."

Doug was in a high school group that was doing some volunteer work for a church, but it was a mile or so away from our house. So the cat didn't belong to someone in the neighborhood. It had obviously been dropped into our car by someone trying to get rid of it, or hoping it would find a home, to see things in the best light.

"It has a funny tail," Denny said. "It's cut off short and hooked at the end, like it was in an accident."

"Or mayhem," I said. "What are we running here—a sanitarium?"

"I think my pie's done," she said.

A shadow moved into the house. I went outside. The scenery had changed again. The blue sky was gone. A raindrop hit my nose. I got the weather panels out of the garage and put them back up.

In the house the serenade had finished. The gentlemen with the long hair had put their instruments in their cases and put on their funny eighteenth-century hats and gone away.

The harmony was broken. But I wasn't sad. Every moment is a beginning.

The pie was good, and we named the kitten Mozart.

Mozart turned out to be intelligent. Whether she actually had the creative impulse, I can't say. Assuming that her artistic efforts were conscious, she was a student of the action school, and her work was strongly suggestive of the later Jackson Pollack.

One of her most stunning productions, which she casually knocked off one day, was a dynamic abstraction done with red Italian wine on a beige nylon carpet.

Being a cat she was of course obliged to work with the materials at hand. The wine, a Chianti, had been given to us for Christmas. It was the sort of object you don't know what to do with. It came in a gallon jug with a thin four-foot neck. We had no place to store it, so we left it in the living room as a conversation piece, though it doubtless inhibited more conversation than it stimulated.

Several times I had noticed Mozart eying the bottle with ominous curiosity. Sometimes she passed at a stray strand of the basket. Once I saw her give it a left hook.

"Someday," I predicted, "Mozart's going to get that bottle."

"Where else can we put it?" Denny asked.

Then one night the muse got into the cat.

I had found out who had been flattening my new rain hat. I usually tossed it aside on the couch, so I'd know where it was in case of rain, and every time I went to get it I found it squashed. All members of the family pleaded not guilty.

I was sitting on the couch one evening when Mozart jumped onto the couch and deliberately climbed up on top of the hat, curling into an oval ball the exact size of the crown. As I watched, too fascinated by this act of self-incrimination to intervene, the crown slowly began to sink. It went down like an elevator, with a hiss of escaping air.

I had to teach her not to do it. I rolled up a section of the newspaper and raised it in menace. She flew off my hat like a missile and bounded into the kitchen. I followed. Cornered in the kitchen, she doubled back. She streaked by my ankles as I made a swipe at her with the rolled-up newspaper. She sprang to a chair and catapulted to the top of the dining room table. I rounded the table. She put on her brakes and went into a treacherous skid. She slid from the table and crashed into the neck of the wine bottle. Over it went.

The neck cracked in two. Wine gushed from the open throat. Great gurgling red cascades of Chianti spilled onto the carpet, spreading outward in a great shapeless stain.

We were paralyzed by the extent of this disaster. No one could move until the beheaded bottle gave up its last red trickle.

As we studied the hideous stain we began to realize that it had a kind of beauty. It was certainly as abstract as some of Pollack's paintings I had seen. At least it had a story to go with it; and I don't believe any of Pollack's reds ever aroused such emotions in me.

Later, Denny tried removing the stain with shampoo. All she did, though, was weaken its message. The stain stayed there until we bought a new carpet. Every time I noticed it I felt stupid about leaving the bottle in the living room and guilty about chasing the cat. For as long as it remained, that stain was my scarlet letter.

By the time Mozart came into the house, Gato was well established. She had had no competition. I wondered whether she would be hostile to this intruder.

Perhaps it was a mark of her character, or of feline character in general, that she seemed to take no notice of Mozart. She was not concerned, nor did she alter her ways. If the kitten offered to play, she simply walked away, or, if necessary, made a feint at her, which was enough to discourage further nonsense.

Mozart soon began to treat Gato in the same way. Thus, in lofty indifference to each other, they were to live together in our house for years.

7

One morning when I had the day free I decided to do the poodles a favor and give them a bath.

"It's ridiculous," I told Denny, "to pay ten dollars each to have a dog washed at the vets. I'll do it myself. Save some money."

She said she was going to be gone for a few hours. "Are you sure you can handle it without help?" she asked.

"Don't worry," I said, "I've washed dogs before."

The last time I'd tried washing two dogs it had turned into a sort of comic opera, and that was years before, when the boys were home, somewhat at my command, and very useful in such an undertaking. Now they were gone—Doug at UCLA, Curt in the Air Force—and I was having to learn all over again how to do things by myself.

Also, that other time we had washed the dogs outdoors, which made it easier for them to get away, but eliminated the potential catastrophe of letting two soapy dogs loose in the house.

That had been when we had Shaggy and her bumptious offspring Blaze. That memorable project had started out well enough. Both Blaze and Shaggy came when I called and stood at my feet wagging their tails. Then they saw one of the boys coming out of the house with a brush and bucket slosh-full of water. I grabbed Blaze just in time, but Shaggy bolted. I realized they were smarter dogs than I had supposed.

We got Blaze washed, but not being used to total submersion, he began to shiver. Doug dried him with a towel and took him into the house. When he brought him out again Blaze was wearing some kind of a striped jersey (I think it was my Portuguese fisherman's shirt) and a familiar looking pair of red Bermuda shorts. I remember that Doug said, "Look, Pa—Maurice Chevalier!"

Shaggy, meanwhile, had taken the road clear around to the other side of the canyon. She sat there howling at us. Blaze got the message and set out in exuberant pursuit. The last we saw of them they were headed over the hill toward the Dalton place.

In a minute or two the phone rang. It was Freddie Dalton, our neighbor across the canyon.

"Are your dogs out?" he asked.

I told him they were, and they were headed for his house. "Well, you'd better come and get 'em," he said, "the one in the red shorts is chasing the other one, and she hasn't got a stitch of clothes on. Heh heh."

This time I wasn't staging any comedy for Dalton. Instead of washing the poodles outdoors I'd use the bathtub, where it would be easy to contain them.

First I got a bar of flea soap and read the directions: "Wet dog thoroughly with warm water. Work up a heavy lather and let remain on for five minutes before rinsing."

I called Jolie first. She came to me obediently, but without any enthusiasm. Her suspicions were aroused. Fortunately, I had never given her a bath in the bathtub before, so she didn't have it figured out. I put her in the tub, into which I had already run three inches of water, and held her down on one side, with her head sticking up, her great dark eyes reproaching me.

"Stay there," I told her, though I don't know what gave me the idea that she would.

I left her looking apprehensive and betrayed, and went to find Beau. As I was coming back with him, I met Jolie trotting through the living room, wet and rebellious. She dashed into the sunroom and took refuge under a rattan chair.

"Come on," I told her. "Out of there. You're going to have a bath."

She backed farther under the chair. I got on my knees and dragged her out with my free arm. She shook herself and sprinkled me liberally. That was when I realized I would have to change into swimming trunks. I shut the dogs in the bathroom and changed.

I put both dogs into the tub. I wet them thoroughly and began to work up a heavy lather. Meanwhile, I was working up a heavy sweat. The bathroom was hot and steamy. I opened the door to let some air in. Beau leaped out of the tub and dashed through the living room. I ran after him. It was at this point that I began to swear.

I caught Beau and put him back in the tub. Again I lathered both dogs. Then I sat on the tub to wait five minutes before rinsing. I wondered how to handle the rinsing. I decided the only thing was for me to get into the tub with the dogs and turn on the shower.

When the five minutes were up I got into the tub and turned on the shower. Foam began streaming off the dogs and down the drain. I heard the phone ring in the bedroom. I got out of the tub. "Stay there," I told the dogs.

It was Dalton. "How about coming over for a swim?" he said.

"I'm in the shower," I said. "With the dogs."

"With the dogs?"

"Yes. We're taking a bath."

I hung up and caught the dogs. They had got out of the tub and were in the living room under chairs. They were both wet and slippery; it was exasperating work. I cursed loudly, which of course didn't make catching the dogs any easier.

Somehow we got through with the shower. Too exhausted to struggle, I let the dogs escape into the sunroom. After I rested and had a glass of beer, as a relaxant, I went after them with towels.

"How did it go?" Denny asked when she came home.

"Nothing to it," I said. "Piece of cake."

She went into the bathroom. "Good Lord!" she cried. "The bathroom's under a foot of water! Not to mention dog hair and soap suds."

I decided to let the vet wash them after that. It was too dangerous sloshing about in a porcelain tub with two animals. I could easily have fallen and broken an arm. Besides, my wife refused to do her share by cleaning up.

Sometimes we go on thinking we failed at something only to find out years later, perhaps by accident, that we succeeded after all, and never knew it.

"Come out here a minute," Denny called from the backyard one morning after our sons had gone away.

How I responded to a call like that depended on the urgency in her tone. Sometimes the cat would have a lizard. Once it was a mockingbird thrashing about in a covered waste basket. Another time it was only a tarantula on the doorstep, a situation which, as a liberated woman, she was quite capable of handling herself.

I found her standing under the deodar tree, looking down.

"The birdhouse finally fell," she said. "It must have been the wind."

Our boys had built two birdhouses and put them up in the deodar a dozen years or so before.

They had spent days and nights in the garage—sawing, planing, hammering, painting. We were surprised and delighted with the results. The houses were true and pretty, with dowels for perches and round holes for doors. One was blue, the other red.

We watched as they climbed the tree, up into the high branches, and nailed the houses in place. It was a good spring day. The boys were agile and excited and the birds kept flying about on reconnaissance. I supposed they could hardly wait to move in.

Spring ended and summer came and vanished and no birds ever moved into the houses. Now and then one of the boys would climb up and peek in, but there was no sign of tenants. I used to have my breakfast in the sunroom and watch the tree, but I never saw a bird so much as look inside one of the houses or sit on a perch.

We got plenty of advice that first spring.

"It's your colors, Jack," a neighbor told me. "They're too bright. You should've painted 'em brown."

"It's probably because the houses are too new," a woman told my wife at a PTA meeting. "Wait till next spring."

"What kind of birds did you have in mind?" Dalton asked.

"Just any birds," I said. "We don't care."

"Your bird," Dalton said, "is just like your housewife. It wants a house that suits its particular needs."

It was the same thing all over again the next spring and the next summer, and year after year, until we all sort of forgot about the birdhouses, or pretended to.

The blue house was the first to come down. It had crashed, empty, when we hired a man to prune the tree, and I had dropped it in the trash.

And now I was looking down at the red house. It was faded and scabrous and askew. I bent over and picked it up and my heart thumped. There was something inside. I wrenched the roof off and there it was, a nest.

"Why the thing's been lived in," I said.

I phoned my son at his Air Force base (he hadn't yet gone to Southeast Asia) to tell him the news, but he was somewhere out on the aircraft line, the duty sergeant told me.

"Any message?" he asked.

"No, I guess not," I said. "I'll try him later."

I didn't want to tell an Air Force sergeant that a birdhouse one of his men had built as a boy had been lived in after all, had sheltered a pair of birds, and their chicks, and helped to put a new generation in the sky.

Maybe I should have. Maybe he would have understood.

8

I had always wanted an Airedale, as unpractical as an Airedale would be in the confinement of the city. When I was a small boy a neighbor had owned one, and I remembered him as the noblest dog I ever knew.

I realized it was foolish for me to buy a dog. I could take my choice of the strays that came to our door almost every day. We had taken in strays before, and would again. I had no interest in breeding pedigreed dogs. What was the point, then, of buying one with papers? I had always liked curs, anyway, and they needed homes.

But I hankered for an Airedale.

One weekend when my wife had driven down to our house in Baja, California, I turned to the classified section of the Sunday paper and found an ad for "Airedale Pups. AKC."

I began to fantasize. Couldn't an Airedale be happy in the city?

I wanted a fairly large dog that would sit by my

chair, take walks with me, heeling, ride beside me
in the car. I wanted one we could take to the house
in Baja, one that would know instinctively how to
deal with snakes and would not be intimidated by
strangers in the night. We had the two poodles, but
I thought of them as my wife's dogs, and so did
they. I wanted a dog that would know it was mine.

How I acted out these fantasies has been described in *Spend All Your Kisses, Mr. Smith.* The
kennel, as readers of that book may recall, was out
in Rosemead, not far from Santa Anita Park. The
house sat back behind a high redwood fence, and
over the fence I could see a big Airedale in the
yard. My blood stirred. I knocked on a gate. The
Airedale barked. It was a deep and resonant sound,
not unpleasant, with neither fear nor malice in it.
It was simply a sound of authority. Other Airedales soon joined him, adding their own somewhat less authoritative notes.

"What is it?" a woman called, and in a moment
she came out of the house and into the yard among
the dogs.

She quieted the dogs and let me in. She said
there were only two pups left of a litter of nine—
a male and a female, not quite four months old.
Being the last of nine, I supposed, they had been
passed over in the draft, so to speak. They were
not, she conceded frankly, of the best show quality, but they were Airedales every inch, and of good
character. And perhaps the male, if I took the
trouble to train his ears, could be shown.

The female was smaller, and she seemed to be
more interested in me than the male was. She trot-

ted over and rubbed against my leg and stayed there, and that was important. I wasn't sure why, but I decided to take the male, although he had all but ignored me, after giving me a brief inspection. Maybe it was because he already had a name, and I liked it.

"We call him Pugsley," the woman said. "You can give him a new name, though. It's just a nickname the kids gave him."

"No, Pugsley it is," I said, thinking it was probably just as unlucky to change a dog's name as a boat's.

We went indoors to close the deal and she showed me Pugsley's family tree. His sire's name was Fleetwood SuperSon, his dame's Fleetwood Sun Maid.

"Fleetwood," she explained, "is the kennel name."

So his real name, I realized, was Fleetwood Pugsley. We started for home in my convertible with Fleetwood Pugsley in the passenger seat; but he preferred the driver's seat. I had a hard time driving and keeping him off me, and I suffered a few misgivings.

More were to come. When I reached our house the cats ran out to greet me, recognizing the sound of the car engine. I got out and walked around to the passenger side to open the door. The cats were at my ankles, unaware of the monstrous surprise about to descend on them.

I tried to shoo them away but they wouldn't go. I opened the door and Fleetwood Pugsley slid from the seat to the street. Mozart flew; Gato hissed,

arched her back, struck out with a paw, and retreated.

Pugsley seemed unperturbed by this reaction.
I took him through the house to the back door,
where the poodles were waiting, yipping in their
usual excitement. Beau fled. Jolie, the braver, bared
her teeth, then followed her fainthearted brother
into the doghouse we'd built them.

Everyone was tense throughout the weekend
except the Airedale. I was anxious; the cats remained surly and alert; the poodles stayed in their
doghouse, surrendering their territory without a
fight. Fleetwood Pugsley appeared curious but at
ease. I knew he was made of the right stuff.

It was in this uneasy peace that my wife found
us when she came home.

I have read in sentimental dog stories that people
can learn character from dogs. I have never really
believed it. Perhaps there is no harm in the idea
that dogs can teach us patience, loyalty and courage, among other virtues. But a dog is a dog and
a man is a man, and they have different kinds of
patience, loyalty and courage. And what may con-
ceivably be a virtue in one is not even logical in the
other. Who can imagine a chaste dog?

In the first few weeks Fleetwood Pugsley did
seem to be teaching my wife and me good manners, although indirectly. He taught Denny, for
example, not to hang her nylons to dry in the
doorway. He did this by tugging on them until she
got the idea. She got the idea after only two pairs.
It was the same method I was using to teach him

how to sit up—repetition. One does a thing over and over until the dog gets the idea, or the person gets the idea, whichever is the pupil.

Sometimes he seemed to be criticizing our taste. We had a yellow upholstered sofa in the living room that had been rather expensive, but once it was home we realized that its abstract pattern was too nervous for us, and its color too neurotic. We couldn't understand what had moved us to buy it, and wondered how to get rid of it without admitting our error.

I don't mean to suggest that Fleetwood Pugsley perceived the problem in an aesthetic sense, but perhaps it isn't impossible. Dogs can't tell yellow from blue, I've read, though I don't see how we can know what colors they see. But a dog with aristocratic lineage might be able to distinguish a nervous pattern from a calm one. In any case, he chewed an arm off the sofa, leaving it beyond repair. Our dilemma was resolved.

He also caused me to give up leaving socks on the floor, a habit of mine that Denny deplored. Either he considered it untidy, or else he fantasized my socks as objects of the chase, being a terrier. He worried them to shreds.

When we acquired the poodles I had had a three-foot fence put up to keep them in. We never allowed our dogs to roam the neighborhood, that being the law. I worried that three feet might not be high enough, but I needn't have. Neither of the poodles ever showed any interest in jumping the fence and challenging the world beyond it.

But the day he turned four months, the Airedale got out. He announced this feat by appearing at the front door and barking to get in. I had no idea how he had gotten out.

I checked the fence. All four gates were shut and latched. It was a puzzle, like a locked-door mystery by Ellery Queen. My theory was that he had pushed the patio chaise longue over to the fence and used it like a ramp. My wife said he had simply jumped the fence. I couldn't believe it.

By then he had learned to operate the revolving cocktail table in the living room and the lazy-Susan pots-and-pans cabinet in the kitchen. He seemed to like the jolly noise the pots and pans made when they spun out on the kitchen floor, and it gave me hope that he was musical.

He tore up the pad of the chaise longue and the seat of the hibiscus chair in the patio. He put three polka dots in the living room carpet and systematically altered the entire backyard, especially my wife's ornamental planted pots. At first the gardener thought my wife was doing it, and was afraid she had lost her mind.

Finally I took Pugsley down to Dr. Morehouse, explaining that I thought he ought to have a "routine checkup," but I really was worried that the dog might have some glandular problem. He seemed hyperactive, at least.

Dr. Morehouse told me we should consider ourselves lucky to have finally gotten an intelligent dog, so late in life.

"He's just exuberant, Jack," he said.

He warned me, though, that I could expect Pugsley to become even more aggressive when the sex drive set in.

I decided that the next thing to be altered at our place would be Fleetwood Pugsley himself.

By the time he was six months old, the Airedale had chewed almost everything in the house but my pliers. As he grew more mature, he no longer chewed aimlessly, but with a purpose.

Systematically, he destroyed the poodles' doghouse. It was large and bulky, and couldn't be taken whole, so he gnawed at it from the edges, the way you nibble on a cracker. This caused the poodles almost constant anguish. They would run into their house to get away from the Airedale, who only wanted to play, cowering inside it like children hiding from an ogre in a Grimm's fairy tale, only to be terrorized by the sound of his molars grinding on their roof.

"How would you like it," my wife asked, "if you heard some monster chewing on your roof?"

I tried to tell her it did no good to think of dogs in human terms. We had no way of knowing what a dog thought under such circumstances, any more than we knew what he thought of Picasso.

I could hardly wait until Pugsley was old enough to be altered, but something came up that caused me to postpone the operation. Actually, he was turning into such a handsome specimen that I thought he might be a show dog after all. I had been invited by the Airedale Association to enter him in the big Airedale Futurity of the following spring, when he would be eligible, and the idea rather excited me.

Of course a show dog can't be altered. And I would have to shape him up. He needed to chew if he was to keep his teeth in good condition. The poodles were helping to keep him lean by playing with him, even if they didn't regard it as play. A healthy Airedale needed something to chase and to harry. I doubted that a bored or idle terrier could be a champion.

I hadn't known there was such a thing as a futurity for Airedales until I got the notice from the association. It wasn't a race, as I might have thought; it was a show. But the top dogs could win some money.

I had no idea of entering Pugsley for the money, though. I just felt that every dog ought to be allowed to discover its own potential and identity as a dog. If Fleetwood Pugsley had the stuff of champions, I didn't want to stand in his way.

The big problem in getting him ready for the futurity was gluing his ears. The woman who had sold him to me at Fleetwood Airedales reminded me of this in a worried note:

"Did you manage to hold Pugsley still long enough to glue his ears? This should be done if he's to be shown."

If an Airedale is to have peaked ears, as a terrier should, the tips must be glued to his forehead for three or four weeks when he's young. Otherwise, the ears will flop like a bloodhound's.

I tried hard to glue his ears. You must apply glue to the ears, then hold them in place with your thumbs for twenty to thirty minutes. The only success I had was in getting one of his ears glued to my pajama top. The longest I ever held the ears in place, by actual count on the digital clock, was seventeen seconds. I thought of trying it when he was asleep, but he never slept when I was watching.

I never did get his ears glued, and had to give up the idea of entering him in the futurity. There was no longer any compelling reason not to have him altered.

9

I did not enjoy making the decision to end Fleetwood Pugsley's sex life before (as far as I knew) it had begun, but I was sure that in the long run it would be the right thing for him as well as for the neighborhood. Shaggy had taught me a lesson, but the owners of male dogs had to take some responsibility too. I had also been sobered by an article in *Business Week:* "Before you join in on the great dog boom that has developed over the past few years," it counseled, "consider the responsibility and substantial cost involved in owning and caring for a dog."

I had already accepted that responsibility; but the magazine suggested that people who already owned dogs ought to consider having them spayed or castrated. I would have said "neutered" myself, as I am somewhat given to euphemisms. I said it to Tinker Belle, at the vet's.

"Do you think it would make the dog unhappy," I asked her, "if I had him neutered?"

"No, Mr. Smith," she said, looking at me frankly with those lavender eyes, "it won't change the dog's personality at all to have him castrated."

I considered it a lesson. In the presence of a sophisticated young woman a man was no longer required to employ euphemisms. Not only that, Tinker Belle almost convinced me, then and there, that the thing should be done. It would make him an easier dog to live with, she assured me.

"And it won't make him unhappy," she said, "because he won't know what he's missing."

That sounded reasonable, but I wondered. Mightn't a male animal thus deprived of his sex glands nevertheless be disturbed by vague promptings and mysterious stirrings, by a sense of mission unaccomplished? But Dr. Morehouse himself erased my doubts.

"Jack," he said, "you'll both be happier."

The article I had read seemed to bear him out. "Most experts agree," it said, "that unless you have a superb breed specimen, you should have your pet spayed or castrated. Neutering can also make your dog a better pet. Male dogs become more docile, get into fewer scrapes and are less inclined to roam. . . ."

It made me feel a bit guilty about owning a pet at all. I suspect the reason most of us own them is that we enjoy their devotion. There was a cartoon in the *New Yorker* some years ago in which a man was sitting in an easy chair and a bird dog of some kind was nuzzling his arm, and the man was saying to his wife, "I think this is the first dog we've had that has—you know—worked out."

The Airedale hadn't exactly worked out, at least not yet. I always wondered if I shouldn't have bought his sister, instead of him. The two of them had been the last of the litter, and I remembered how the female had come and stood at my knee and wouldn't go away. Obviously she had been instantly drawn to me. Pugsley had come up to look me over, let me pat him once on the head, and trotted off looking for mischief. But I took him instead of her because he was like me—curious, independent, restless and exploratory. And male.

I realized, of course, that I was a victim of my own male chauvinism. A man should not buy a dog like himself to please his vanity. He should buy a dog with the qualities he looks for in a wife—a dog to improve his years. Patient, faithful, devoted and brave. But dogs like that are hard to find (not to mention wives).

With Pugsley supposedly somewhat calmed down, but still young, our daughter-in-law Gail tried to get me to put him in a dog obedience school. She was taking her dog to night school in a public park, and thought it was helping. So one evening I went with her to check it out. I would no more have put Pugsley into a school I hadn't looked into than I would have put my daughter into a finishing school I hadn't looked into, if I'd had a daughter.

I didn't take him with me. I reasoned that if he didn't like it he wouldn't go again, and if he did like it, he might not want to leave.

I picked up my daughter-in-law and her dog at her house and we drove to the park. Her dog was a toy-size female, a mixture of fox terrier and possibly part Chihuahua. She was an appealing little mutt with a small head and large eloquent eyes. Her name was Sadie, which fit her very well.

The park was cold. I would have been warm enough if I'd brought the dog, as the owners, I soon saw, were required to walk their dogs around the outdoor basketball court, teaching them how to heel.

I sat on a bench, buried my hands in the pockets of my corduroy coat and turned up the collar. There were twenty-six owners and dogs; young and old; a few more women than men. Some of the dogs were hard to identify. Half a dozen German shepherds, three or four Dobermans, a beagle, a boxer pup with its ears taped, a wirehaired fox terrier, a couple of Irish setters, a pointer, a Labrador, a cockapoo pup and a number of unclassifiable refugees from the dog pound.

A young woman stood at the center of the court shouting instructions. "Forward!" she shouted, and the owners and dogs began walking clockwise around the court. "Stop!" she shouted. Most of the dogs miraculously stopped and sat, as they were supposed to. However, the wirehaired terrier ran forward and snapped at the tail of a German shepherd, which swung around to defend himself but ended up pawing at the air as his mistress yanked him up by the collar. In an instant half a dozen of the more aggressive dogs were barking and straining at their leashes.

"When your dog goes after another dog," shouted the instructor, "you can't just pull him back gently. You have to give him a real yank. You have to mean it. Some dogs just have to show their manliness. Especially the males."

It was a pretty sexist remark, I thought, but since my dog wasn't present I decided to let it pass.

"Forward!" she shouted, and order was soon restored.

Every owner, I noticed, had his own way of coaxing obedience from his dog. One young woman, every time she passed me, said "Heel— damn you!" She said it under her breath, but I could read her lips.

"Come on, Iris," said a man with an Irish setter as they passed. "Heel up, and close your mouth."

"Get your tail up," said the man with the beagle. "Come on. This is supposed to be fun."

"Fast!" shouted the instructor, and everyone broke into a trot. My daughter-in-law, I noticed, had complete control over Sadie, but they seemed to be running faster than the others. "It's because we're both so little," she explained later. "Even at 'walk' we have to trot to keep up."

Suddenly there was another commotion. The wirehair again. "Stop!" shouted the instructor. She strode over to the wirehair and took his leash and gave him an authoritative jerk. "Heel!" she commanded, and led him out on the court. "You have to get their attention," she pointed out. "You have to mean it."

I decided against enrolling Pugsley in the obedience class. I wasn't in shape for it, for one thing. And I wasn't sure obedience was what I wanted out of him. He was a free spirit.

10

We hadn't had a more exciting weekend up on Mt. Washington since the brush fire that took eight houses back in the late '50s.

It began quietly enough, earlier in the week, when a neighbor of ours on the other side of the hill, Dan Trimmer, looked out his window and saw a strange bird. As Lee Trimmer, his wife, recalled it later, trying to get his exact words, he called to her and said, "There's a dopey-looking bird out here."

Dan Trimmer had been ailing and was in bed on a small porch, or sunroom, off the Trimmer living room. It is a small two-level house, perched on a steep side of the hill among trees and chaparral. Bird life is abundant, and Trimmer had been entertaining himself by watching through the window.

Mrs. Trimmer got to the window in time to see the bird and realized it was one she had never seen before. She wasn't what you would call a hard-core bird-watcher, but fortunately she was interested enough to own a copy of *Peterson's Field Guide*. Even so, she was too busy at the moment to look up the new bird, and he had been hanging around for two or three days before she finally decided to check him out.

The bird was a hummer, which was obvious, but what made him different, among other things, was his bill. It was broad and red. Indeed, he looked very much like the bird whose picture she found on page 166: a male broad-billed hummingbird.

"*Cynanthus latirostris*," the book said, "Male: Dark green above and below with a blue throat (bird looks all black in distance). Bill bright red, with black tip. Voice: A chatter. . . . Hum of male is higher pitched than other species; has zing of a rifle bullet."

One thing gave her pause. The bird wintered in Mexico, and was not listed as inhabiting California at all. Even so, Mrs. Trimmer felt quite sure of the identification. Book in hand, she telephoned the Audubon Society.

"I have a broad-billed hummingbird outside my window on Mt. Washington," she told them.

It would be hard to overstate the impact of Mrs. Trimmer's discovery on the inner circle of the Audubon, and eventually on the tranquility of her own household and neighborhood. Mrs. Trimmer's first call came from Jean Brandt, a mainstay of the local Audubon and a birder of unquestioned integrity. Mrs. Brandt verified Mrs. Trimmer's report by phone, then got in her car at once and drove to Mt. Washington to see for herself. The Trimmer house is not easy to find, and when you find the address the house is still hard to find, being somewhat concealed, like a birdhouse in a tree; but Jean Brandt, I'm sure, would have brooked no obstacle in her quest. She was in the vanguard of a pilgrimage, for the fact is that the broad-billed hummingbird had never before been seen in Los Angeles.

I am pleased to say that Mrs. Brandt suggested to Mrs. Trimmer, with whom I was not then acquainted, that she telephone me. "He'd like to know," she said, or something like that.

Mrs. Trimmer did phone me, but by the time I could finish up my work and get over to her house I found that a dozen of the best-known birders in the West had been there first. Mrs. Trimmer had decided to put out a guest book, and it was already signed by Arnold Small, Shumway Suffel, Charles and Elsie Bernstein and other illustrious birders.

"You wouldn't believe it, who's been here," said Mrs. Trimmer. "My husband said, 'Who's coming over—a bunch of little old ladies?' Well, they've been mostly men. And such nice people."

"Is he still around?" I asked. "The bird?"

"Oh, yes. Every twenty minutes."

The hummer would appear, Mrs. Trimmer promised me, at the feeder hanging just outside her kitchen window. "You'll hear him. He makes a lot of noise."

In a minute or two I heard a zing and some chatter and there he was, not feeding, but hovering and looking in the window.

"He has to check you out," said Mrs. Trimmer.

Evidently satisfied, the bird settled into the ring under the feeder, stuck his long red bill into the cup, and drank.

That was only Friday. All day Saturday and Sunday the birders came, and Mrs. Trimmer was advised to expect some from as far away as Santa Barbara and San Francisco.

The wonderful thing about it for me, as I saw it, was that it would force the Audubon experts to review an unusual sighting of my own. Some time previously I had casually mentioned seeing a grackle fly over my birdbath, and had been much ridiculed for it. No grackle, it was stated, had ever been seen west of the Mississippi River. Now that they had seen Mrs. Trimmer's broad-tailed hummingbird on Mt. Washington, mightn't they feel obliged, in the best interests of birding, to reconsider my grackle? (I will deal later on with the outcome of this now celebrated case.)

Not long after Mrs. Trimmer's hour in the sun, I came close to achieving my own celebrity. It happened one weekend when my wife was out of town.

I spent most of the weekend reading, writing letters, and watching birds. I had hung a hummingbird feeder from an eave just outside our glass door, and I placed my rattan rocking chair a few feet away, so that I would notice it when a bird came to drink of the pink syrup. I was hoping to attract Mrs. Trimmer's broad-billed hummer, or maybe something even rarer.

On Saturday I saw nothing but Anna's hummingbirds. They are pretty enough, with their green backs and neon red throats, but they are quite common here, nothing to make a man leap from his chair and phone the Audubon.

It was Sunday, slightly after noon, when I thought I saw something different. I got up and stood closer to the window. We had a solar film on our windows at the time (to cut the sun's heat) and it had the effect of turning the outside surface into a mirror. Thus, the birds couldn't see in, and were not frightened away. There was no doubt of it, this bird was something else. My pulse quickened as I got my eyes into focus and saw that he was reddish brown, not green, and his throat was a fiery orange-red.

He was gone before I could find him in my guide; but he was listed, and the description left me with no doubt. He was a rufous hummingbird *(Selasphorus rufus)*—an adult male. "No other N. American hummingbird has a rufous back," the book said. "Upper parts bright non-iridescent red-brown, throat flaming orange-red."

My first thought was to telephone the Audubon at once so they could put out an alert. Dozens of birders would soon be tramping through the house, but it was my duty. First, I wanted to be absolutely sure. With the grackle question still moot, I couldn't afford a blot on my credibility. They would say I had cried wolf too many times.

I decided to call Chuck Bernstein, who was then still leading the December birdwalk at Descanso Gardens; but he didn't answer. I'd have to wait and catch him at work on Monday.

I saw the rufous several times again. Once, in his absence, an incredible thing happened. A gorgeous orange bird flew down from the palm tree, lighted on top of the hummingbird feeder and tried to get his beak into one of the tiny feeding holes, upside down. Of course he couldn't, and succeeded only in falling off, over and over again, and making a fool of himself.

I looked him up in my field guide and decided he must be a Lichtenstein's oriole, though rather small for the species.

The next day I phoned Bernstein. "Is the rufous hummingbird very rare in Los Angeles?" I asked him.

"No," he said. "It isn't."

"Well, what about the Lichtenstein's oriole?"

"Jack," he said, "no Lichtenstein's oriole has ever been seen west of the Rio Grande."

Well, at least the Rio Grande was closer than the Mississippi, but I decided not to mention that I'd seen one.

I was happy to let someone else have the glory.

11

I wanted to raise my Airedale as a normal dog, without urban neuroses, but I did decide to teach him to restrain his barking. I knew I might be reproached on the grounds that barking is a dog's birthright. But in the city a man's neighbors are entitled to peace and quiet, especially in the dead of night.

Fleetwood Pugsley was not really an indiscriminate barker; his trouble was that he failed to bark at the right time more often than he barked at the wrong time. He was extremely fond of people. A man could climb the fence in a fright mask, with a case of burglar's tools, and provoke nothing more from Fleetwood than an affectionate whine and a kiss on the neck. On the other hand, he had an unerring eye and nose for any other dog, no matter how small and distant, and would set to barking raucously the moment another dog entered his territory, which he evidently conceived to be not only our yard but also the entire canyon below us and the road to the top of the hill.

I often heard him let loose an unearthly salvo and would rush from the house expecting to find him surrounded by coyotes, only to see that the object of his outburst was some tiny Chihuahua being walked on a string by one of the neighbors on the hill road a quarter of a mile away. Why such a tidbit should arouse his carnal or territorial instincts, I couldn't imagine.

You might think it would not be easy to alter the barking pattern of a dog like that. My approach was simple. Whenever he barked, I would yank open the door to the dog yard to catch him in the act, and shout "Quiet!" Only the one word, always the same.

Usually this stopped him. He understood the word and wanted to cooperate. However, if the dog he was barking at was deceptively small—let's say a Scottie—he was not so easily restrained. I was then obliged to pick up a stick I kept handy and rap him with it. He didn't like it, and would take cover in the hibiscus tree.

Pugsley was not a stupid dog, and responded quite well to the program. In time, all I had to do was shout "Quiet!" from inside the house and he swallowed his noise. It was a pitiful sound he uttered when he swallowed a bark. It was as if the sound had already been made inside him and he had to get it out even though his brain said stop. It could be heard blowing around deep inside him, like wind in a cave; it seemed to hurt him physically. He writhed and worked his jaws and finally shuddered, and the sound came up in his throat and died out in a deep groan, like a phonograph record when the power is turned off.

So I had the thing pretty well in hand. But my system didn't work well early in the morning. He never missed the Dawn Patrol. That was the core of the problem. My neighbor George seemed to enjoy his early-morning sleep the most, and the dog was always up and about at first light, barking at moles, skunks, raccoons and other nocturnal creatures that were just knocking off for the night.

He often woke me long before my own alarm went off. I tried yelling "Quiet!" from bed, without getting up, making it loud enough to carry through the house and out to the yard. That was unsatisfactory on two counts: it failed to quiet the dog and it woke my wife.

One early morning when Pugsley started barking, I got up and walked through the house in the dark, avoiding the furniture by memory, and yanked open the backyard door.

"Quiet!" I shouted. He barked. I leaped out, slamming the door behind me, and grabbed the stick.

He scooted toward the hibiscus tree, swallowing great gulps of sound.

I turned to go back inside. The door was locked. I had forgotten to release the night latch again.

I don't know which bothered George the most— an Airedale barking at dawn, or a man in a nightshirt calling plaintively for his sleeping wife to let him back in the house.

How a man raises his children seems to be regarded in our country as his own business, but not how he raises his dog.

After publishing a report on my method for teaching Fleetwood Pugsley not to bark, thinking it might help other owners, I was inundated with advice—most of it useless and some of it surly.

"Have you no sensitivity toward animals?" wrote one critic. "Your best friend is bored and lonesome and being incarcerated all day and night in a yard. Have you nothing in the way of toys and/or love to entertain him with? What about long walks in the woods?"

Another reproach came on the letterhead of an attorney-at-law, and it gave a moment's alarm. I wondered if I had done something actionable. But he was only writing as a citizen:

"If you have real concern for your neighbors and the barking problem," he said, "you would bring your dog inside at night. Neither you nor any other dog owner has any business leaving a dog outside to disturb the neighborhood."

Another woman advised me that the way to keep a dog from barking was to shake a can full of pennies at him, "meanwhile shouting 'No!' in your most stentorian voice."

Not only did I doubt that shaking a can full of pennies would quiet my Airedale, I thought it would almost certainly arouse my neighbors even more than a barking dog would, and contribute to the neighborhood legend that I'm not all there.

Bill Downey, the outdoors writer, took me to task for trying to discipline my dog with "the lowest common denominator—a stick." He held that barking is a dog's therapy; a dog has to bark the way a man has to have a martini. Exercise, he suggested, would do much more to keep a dog from barking than lectures.

On the other hand, Downey recalled an ingenious friend who attacked the ancient problem with modern technology. This fellow had three coon dogs, which are noisy by profession, and he hated to dash out in socks and nightshirt to quiet them at two or three o'clock in the morning when, as Downey put it, "the frost has silvered the grass." So he laid electrical wires in the earth of the dog pen and connected them to a contact box beside his bed, from where he could then control the flow of electricity by pressing a button. When the dogs barked, he could shock them into silence without leaving the warm embrace of his electric blanket.

A wicked plan at best, it failed predictably in actual practice. Downey's friend put it to the test that first night at about eleven o'clock, when his hounds began to bark. He pushed the button. Hearing the chorus of yelps that followed, however, he got the impression that one of the dogs was yelping in soprano, and in English at that.

Downey's friend dashed out in his socks to find that not only were his three hound dogs up on top of the doghouse, but also his wife, in an especially bad mood, I imagine. She worked late as a waitress and had set the dogs to barking when she entered the yard with a sackful of leftover bones.

Downey's friend would have been better off shaking a can of pennies at those hounds.

12

One Saturday the Daltons came over to watch a rerun of *The Birds* on our TV. They had seen it on their set a year or two earlier, but they hadn't had a color set then, and Dalton wanted to see it in color. It was Mrs. Dalton who had resisted getting a color set. She was afraid her husband would spend too much time watching football and old movies.

I remembered that *The Birds* hadn't been acclaimed by the critics as one of Hitchcock's best, but I had liked it. The theme, while improbable, was provocative enough to anyone who lived among wild birds, as we do on the hill, and knew so little about them. Something gets into the birds in the movie (it is never explained) and suddenly they turn on people—attacking, maiming, even killing. It is a horror film, but done with Hitchcock's usual class and fine-tuned suspense.

Dalton was a professor at the University of Southern California, but certainly not in ornithology, so birds were merely his hobby and, like me, he was a novice.

He had been watching them from his pool deck, and was becoming a bit tedious on the subject of their behavior, but otherwise he knew no more about birds than I did. Lately we had been phoning one another when we thought we saw a stranger, and it was rather fun.

One reason he wanted to see *The Birds* again was that he had seen something that alarmed him. "We've got a whole telephone line full of birds over here," he said. "Must be a couple hundred of 'em. You ever seen anything like that?"

He described the birds. Brownish, with a black face and a very high crest and yellow-tipped wings. I happened to know what they were because we had them every year, and I had looked them up in my guide book.

"They're waxwings," I told him. "You've got nothing to worry about. They'll go away. Hold on a minute."

I got my guide and read to him: "A common winter resident, sometimes remaining until May. Usually occur in flocks and while in flight remarkable for the military precision of their movements."

"That's them," he said. "Military precision. They remind me of fascist brownshirts."

In the movie, birds begin making assaults on people, as if in revenge for a millennium of being hunted and killed and eaten. They attack individually, like kamikazes, and in squadrons. The people in the movie are startled and terrified by this inexplicable departure from the normal order of things. When the movie ended we were silent for a while. I started to make a drink. Then Denny said she thought the blonde, Tippy Hedren, was very good, reminded her of Katharine Hepburn. That broke the ice.

"It's Hitchcock's way," I said, "of showing what we're really like. He shows us how horrible the human race can be by having animals act like us. Turning themselves into armies and making war."

"Maybe it could happen," Dalton said. He was still worried about his waxwings.

Sunday morning when I went out to get the paper the telephone line was full of birds. Three hundred, I guessed, twittering ominously. They looked unfriendly and restless. I picked up the paper and went inside.

It was only a movie, I told myself.

Of course I was not really disturbed or alarmed by the movie, though Hitchcock had made it seem possible enough; but it was only his imagination and magic at work. I soon realized that even the waxwings were harmless, their only vice being that they liked to overindulge on our fermented cotoneaster berries and get falling down drunk.

Nevertheless, that next Halloween night, faced with the things that happened at our door, I couldn't help thinking again of Hitchcock and *The Birds*. I have no superstitious fears about Halloween, knowing it is nothing but a children's holiday evolved from an ancient Druid harvest festival, but our Halloween that year was unnerving.

There are some days on which occult forces seem to be at work. People act oddly, and animals intrude unnaturally into human affairs. I should have known that such a day was at hand when Dr. Reap phoned at half-past seven in the morning. Reap is a neighbor of ours, living just up the hill, and was our family doctor for many years. He hadn't yet retired then, but had been easing up, and at last was taking time for things that interested him besides his patients.

"We have two nesting parrots," he said.

It occurred to me that he was finally cracking up. "Well," I said, "we've got finches nesting on the front porch again."

"But these are parrots," he said.

"Parrots aren't uncommon hereabouts," I told him. "They're escaped pets, you know. They're not native. They're exotics, imported from South America or somewhere. But they escape, or people get tired of them and turn them out."

"But these are nesting."

"Well, that's natural."

"But how can an exotic bird find another exotic bird, of the opposite sex, in Los Angeles?"

Dr. Reap is that way. He always has to know the answer to everything. In that way he's like Dalton—and like me, for that matter.

"I'll come up later and have a look," I said.

I didn't tell him that the reason I hadn't sounded too excited about his parrots was that I was jealous. I'd heard other reports of parrots on the hill, but we'd never had any. That's why I knew so much about them. I'd seen an article in the paper about imported parrots escaping and going feral in Los Angeles, and read every word. Dalton was always bragging about his raccoons. What a great thing it would be to tell him we had parrots!

I had a strenuous schedule that day and didn't get home until after six o'clock. The house was dark. I remembered it was Denny's dancing class night. There was a basket of chocolate bars on the dining room table for trick or treat. The little beggars would be on the doorstep any minute. I was worried about the finches. They were in one of Denny's hanging plants near the door and I was afraid that the children, coming and going and squealing trick or treat, might cause them to abandon the eggs. But there was nothing to be done. We always stayed home on Halloween and coped. One couldn't turn the children away.

I no more than got my necktie off than I heard them scuffling up the steps and shrieking, "Trick or treat!" I opened the door to face a sawed-off Batman, a midget Dracula, a skeleton, a clown, and a Frankenstein's monster who looked big enough to be Boris Karloff himself. I dropped a candy bar in each of their sacks.

"You're going to ruin your teeth," I told them.

The clown said, "We only get to do this once a year."

"You have a point," I conceded.

When I shut the door I saw something flutter across the living room. My heart thumped. A bat? It flew back the other way and landed on a curtain rod. It wasn't a bat; it was one of our nesting finches. It must have flown in when I went to get the candy.

It flew into a lamp, then into a window, then lighted, breathing heavily, on a chair. I tried to catch it. It fluttered off in panic.

"Now what am I going to do with you?" I asked it.

"Trick or treat!"

I opened the door. It was a lion, another skeleton, a man with a bird's head, a Barbie Doll, and a record player with an on-off button and a turntable for a stomach. I gave them each a chocolate bar and shut the door.

I wanted a drink, but I knew I would need all my wits and coordination if I were to catch the bird. I opened three windows, took the screens off and tried to chase it out. It flew against the closed windows, avoiding the ones I had opened.

I cursed my wife for being at dancing class. What kind of a dance was more important than catching a bird? The bird flew down to the floor, exhausted, and incredibly I caught it in my hands. I took it to an open window, thrust my hands through, and let it go. It flew back in.

At that moment my wife came home. "What in the world are you doing?" she said.

"I am trying to catch this bird," I explained.

The bird was perched on a lamp, out of reach. "You have to get a stick it can perch on," I said, "then put it out the window."

"Wait a minute," she said.

She went to a corner and picked up a thing she had bought at the Mt. Washington rummage sale. It was a wooden cane with a basket around the shaft below the handle, the shaft of the cane piercing the basket at the center. I had given it a great deal of thought without being able to imagine any possible use for it whatever. She had put it in the corner and as far as I knew she had never looked at it again.

She held the handle end up toward the lamp. The bird hopped off the lamp to the cane. Denny moved slowly to the open window, lowered the cane and stuck it outside. The bird slid off and flew away.

"There," she said. "That's what it's for."

13

If Fleetwood Pugsley hadn't barked one morning, we might have missed one of the great moments of our years on Mt. Washington.

It had dawned hot, and I was up early, as usual, making a pot of coffee in the kitchen, when the Airedale began barking in an urgent way that meant something extraordinary was up. It was not the tone he used on other dogs.

I looked out the window and saw him standing up at the fence, his paws on the pickets, his shoulders well above the top. He was quite capable of jumping it, and would do so as soon as it occurred to him, or there was a compelling reason.

He was looking down on our second level, above the canyon, and I looked down and saw a coyote on the lawn. I caught my breath. He was beautiful. I think that's what astonished me the most; not simply seeing a coyote in our yard, four miles from the City Hall, but finding him so beautiful.

Having lived in the San Joaquin Valley as a boy, I had seen several live coyotes at a distance. I had also seen the carcasses that used to festoon the barbed wire fences for miles along side roads, thousands of them hanging ingloriously by their tails—dead soldiers in their war with the livestock men.

Nobody sees many coyotes these days. They are shy and cunning and rarely let themselves be seen. I had never been so close to one except a miserable few in pens.

The one in our yard looked fit. His coat and tail were luxuriant, his ears alert. He swung his head toward the Airedale, almost fraternally, and then foraged over the lawn with an air of arrogance, rooting and sniffing.

I wanted to shout to my wife to get up but was afraid I'd scare him off. Then his mate appeared. She climbed up out of the canyon with a quick silent grace and loped over the lawn to his side.

I shouted, no longer able to keep so marvelous an event to myself. Denny came padding out of the bedroom on the double. She was used to early reveilles and alarms.

"Quick," I told her, "get your camera."

In the back of my mind a vision of triumph was growing. For years I had envied Dalton his wildlife, just across the canyon. He had even found opossums in his garage. Garter snakes came to his back door. Raccoons went night swimming in his pool. He could hear them diving in at night. But unless I was mistaken, he had never had a coyote.

Prestige on Mt. Washington is not measured by the car in your garage but by the degree of rusticity you are able to cultivate in your life-style. The summer Dalton had the resident raven he was harder than usual to live with. I tried to deflate him by telling him it was only a crow, but he called it a raven and started quoting Poe's poem. Once when we were sitting by the pool there was a rapping at his gate and he went and talked to someone for a moment and came back and said, " 'Twas some visitor, and nothing more."

Our high-water mark was the year we had the skunks and the owl. We've neither of us ever had a king snake. King snakes are No. 1.

Denny was at the window with her little snapshot camera. The coyotes moved toward the edge of the canyon.

"Hurry," I told her.

"They're moving!"

The coyotes slipped into the canyon. "Oh, God," I said, "we'll never be able to prove it."

We ran out of the house and down to the lawn. I saw the coyotes on the other side of the canyon in the poison oak.

"There!"

"Where?"

"Never mind where. Just shoot."

She began snapping away, but by then the coyotes were far up the other side, and mostly hidden in the bush. I knew it would be a miracle if we could find them in the pictures.

That afternoon the Daltons asked us over for a party by their pool. At that time we didn't think we could have a pool ourselves; geologists had told us our soil was too unstable.

"You had much wildlife this summer?" I asked him, leading up to the coyotes.

"Oh, hell yes," he said. "We get raccoons all the time. They like to swim at night, you know."

"How about coyotes?"

"Coyotes? Well, I did see one once. Just a glimpse. Down by the road. They don't like to be seen."

"We had two this morning," I said, "on our lawn."

It stunned him. "Well," he said when he recovered, "I doubt if they'll be back. They were probably thirsty and were hoping you had a pool."

Of course the pictures didn't turn out.

One evening two or three weeks after we saw the coyotes, we were having an early dinner at our table with the Daltons. It was just after dark. Suddenly the Airedale began to bark in that frantic way—half fear, half wild longing—an atavistic sound that interrupted our dinner talk and left us staring at each other like people in a jungle movie when some eerie night scream chills their bones.

"It's our coyotes back," I said, feeling a thrill. We wouldn't have to get a picture to prove it this time.

"Coyotes!" Mrs. Dalton said.

I got up from the table and flipped a wall switch. Light flooded the backyard, reaching just far enough to give a luminous substance to the shapes on the lower level. They were both there, the male and his mate. Their coats were thick and lustrous, their ears and tails magnificent. They stood quite still, their eyes burning with our light.

"They're shepherd dogs," Dalton scoffed.

"I know a coyote," I said, "when I see one."

Suddenly the male swung away. He loped over the lawn and vanished in the canyon. The female followed. In a moment we were back at the table, looking at the Los Angeles City Hall, pale green in the dark sky, and the luminous towers of the downtown skyline.

"I say they were dogs," said Dalton.

We had heard coyotes on Mt. Washington when we first moved to the hill, but these were the first we had seen. Some years we hadn't even heard any, and we assumed they had finally lost their niche in the hill's ecology.

This year was vintage. I didn't know how many there were besides our pair, but sometimes we heard them yipping in the distance, as if there were a pack of them. Somewhere close by, we knew, they must live and breed and raise their pups. Few of my friends believed, however, that we had really seen coyotes in our backyard. Dalton wouldn't even believe his eyes.

Thinking I might get some scientific support, I phoned the Natural History Museum one morning and asked to speak to someone who could help me with coyotes. In a moment a man came on the line.

"Kiowas?" he said. "You've got the wrong department. Just a second. I'll transfer you to the man who can tell you all about Kiowas."

"No, no. Not Kiowas," I said. "Coyotes."

It put me in mind of a correspondence I had had not long before with an anthropologist out at California State L.A. We exchanged three postcards on the subject of "crows" before we discovered that I was talking about birds and she was talking about Indians.

In a moment another man came on the line. "Invertebrate zoology," he said. "Can I help you?"

My mind raced back to high school zoology. I had barely squeezed through.

"The coyote's not an invertebrate, is it?" I said.

"Oh, no. I should think not."

"Then I've got the wrong department."

Everyone was quite courteous, though, and in a moment I got a curator named Don Patten who was not only in mammals, but happily was a neighbor of ours. He lived on the other side of the hill.

He said he hadn't heard or seen any coyotes, but he had seen plenty of raccoons and opossums, and skunks that came right up on his porch.

One night not long after he had moved in, he said, he was sleeping on the floor and woke up to find an animal walking on him. He had a moment's terror.

"I thought it was a rat. But then I saw it in the moonlight. It was a baby 'possum. It had got in through a hole in the screen."

I told Dalton my tale. If I could believe a mammalogist who was awakened by baby 'possums walking on him in the moonlight, he might believe my coyotes.

14

A tragic little drama was played out late one June on our front porch.

Finches had nested on the porch before, but we had never been sure whether any of the chicks had been hatched and made it out of the nest, and we hadn't seen any nests for two or three years. Dozens of cats were at large in the neighborhood, including our own, and the porch was a very small place for birds and cats to co-exist. One or another of the cats was usually there, waiting for a chance to slip inside the house.

The year before, Denny had hung some potted plants from the porch beams, and it may have been these that brought the finches back. It was in May that we first saw them, a pair of house finches, or linnets, shuttling in and out of the porch, their terminal being one of the hanging pots. They soon had a nest the size of a soup cup, and from then on, for the next two weeks or so, the female was in residence.

We were involved. I don't tramp out into the wilds to interfere with nature's structure, but when a creature comes to my door without malicious intent, and is neither venomous nor rabid, it is entitled to my hospitality.

At first, every time one of us walked out on the porch the bird flew away. We used the back door when possible and tried to keep peddlers and visitors off the porch. One Saturday morning I had had to repulse an evangelist. When I opened the door at his knock I saw that the nesting bird was flapping about, bravely trying to frighten him away from the nest.

"Do you know God's Word?" the visitor asked.

"Yeah, verily," I said, "the sparrow hath found a house—and you just scared her out of it."

He gave up on me and went on down the street, not quite in a straight line. They don't like it when you quote Scripture back at them.

Later I saw that the bird had settled back on the nest.

It was the cats that worried me. As I say, they used to loiter on the porch, which ordinarily was their privilege, Gato usually sacking out in a potted succulent on the floor and Mozart on the lower shelf of a metal serving cart Denny had made into a planter. Sometimes I saw them looking up at the nest, and making, I assumed, their calculations.

Then one day when the bird was out we looked in the nest and saw four eggs. "I think they're going to make it," I said.

Two days later we came home and found the bird gone and the nest askew. One egg was left.

There were bits of debris on the porch under the nest, and one small feather.

"The cats," I said, angry but knowing there was no point in anger. But I couldn't see how they did it, unless one had jumped to the top of the serving cart, and from there to the nest, giving it a swipe and tumbling out the eggs. It looked possible. The agility of cats is legendary.

"But there's no sign of broken eggs," Denny pointed out.

"What other explanation is there?" I asked.

I phoned Chuck Bernstein, my Audubon contact, and told him what I suspected.

"Jack," he said, "bell those cats."

"I have enough trouble with the cat people as it is," I told him.

"Which side are you on?"

I needed impartial professional help. You couldn't trust the cat people and you couldn't trust the bird people. Each blamed the other's darlings. I phoned the Natural History Museum and told the story to Ken Stager, then the senior curator of ornithology.

"Do you have scrub jays?" he asked.

Yes, I told him, we had scrub jays but they usually stayed in the backyard, where for years they had been at war with the cats. They were fearless. It was great sport to see them dive-bomb the cats and veer away from those flashing wicked claws, like flying matadors. Once or twice, though, I had found a blue feather or two, and guessed some jay had worked too close to the horns, and finally bought it, or had a close call. But I had never actually seen a cat catch one.

"It could have been the jays," said Stager. "They'll clean out a nest like that."

I might have written it off as one of those things beyond human influence, but then the linnets came 'back for another try. Incredibly, they built another nest in the same place. The eggs were laid and the female took up residence, not six feet above the cats.

I moved the serving cart. If it was the cats, they wouldn't have it as a launching pad. I considered belling them until the birds were fledged. But if the jays were indeed the villains, then temporarily the cats were on my side—the first line of defense. If I belled them, the jays could attack the nest without fear. I wondered how God handled such dilemmas.

Then one morning Denny dashed in from the porch in much excitement. The eggs were hatched. Then the crisis. It would be two tense weeks before the little ones flew.

The nestlings hadn't flown yet when we went away for a long weekend at our house in Baja. We drove away reluctantly, leaving the nest without our protection in those first few perilous weeks of life.

We expected that when we came home we would find either that the four chicks had fledged and flown, or that the cats or blue jays had struck again, leaving nothing but a torn nest and scattered feathers.

But they were still in the nest, all four. With their scrawny necks, frowzy heads and toothless maws they looked more like one hundred-year-old men than new birds. Below them, on the porch floor, Mozart waited in patient blood thirst. We took her in for the night. Gato was out of sight. She had been going down into the canyon to hunt for bigger game.

The next morning Denny went out for the paper and saw one of the chicks on the floor of the porch. The door was open; Mozart got out. Denny shrieked. The bird took off. All this happened before I could get there.

"Did you see it go!" I cried.

The bird had flown straight across the street, low and wobbly, and crash-landed in a bank of ivy. Not good, but not any worse than Kitty Hawk, either. We looked into the nest. Only two were left. Evidently one had taken off on the dawn patrol.

It was the start of an exciting morning. We got Mozart back in. I pulled a stool in front of the window so I could keep an eye on the nest while I drank my coffee and scanned the paper.

In a few minutes the parent birds showed up. They stunted around the porch, landing and taking off, landing and taking off, while the two remaining offspring stood on the edge of the nest, trying to get up enough nerve to go. Suddenly one fell away, came close to a crash, and then was off across the street to a tree. Bravo!

Then I saw the skunk. He simply came walking up the sidewalk as if he were on his way to school, and turned into our flower bed. Did skunks eat birds? I didn't know. I knew what they did do, though.

Mozart hunkered down inside the door, crazy to get out. Would the cat drive the skunk away? Would it provoke the skunk to use its ultimate weapon?

I heard shrill cries and two jays flew onto the porch, hanging in the air near the nest. "Get out!" I shouted through the window. Jays, I knew, were as fearless as badgers; it was almost impossible to scare them away from their prey.

I scouted through the house, looking for a weapon. Behind the bar I found my grandson's broomstick horse. Just the thing. It had a plastic horse's head and a jingle bell. I imagined that, swooping through the air, it would frighten almost anything.

I opened the door to attack the jays. The cat leaped out. Mrs. Johnson from down the street was standing on the sidewalk with her grandson.

"You've got a skunk," she said.

"I know," I said, dropping the horse and going after the cat. I came up on her from behind and got her with one hand around her neck and the other in front of her hindquarters and put her back in the house. The jays flew. The skunk, thank God, was unperturbed.

The linnets came back, trying to get the last bird out of the nest.

He was in no hurry. It was amazing how much neater he looked than he had the night before, like a scruffy schoolboy who has got a haircut and put on a suit for graduation.

He stood on the edge of the nest, finding a dozen things to do instead of going. He fanned out his wings like a poker hand; he picked at imaginary lice; he cheeped. I had been the same way the first time I ever dived off the ten-foot board. Then he fell, only to land in another flower pot below. His parents put on a frenzied demonstration.

I shouted "Go! Go! Go!"

He went.

The skunk hung around for half an hour, then waddled off. I let Mozart out. She jumped out the door, skidded to a stop, and then relaxed. She knew it was over. She had been outmaneuvered.

Suddenly everything was quiet. The nest was empty. The jays were gone. The linnets were gone. The skunk was gone. I had demonstrated that in the urban jungle a man must sometimes turn his own hand to the balancing of nature. All it requires is intelligence, courage, compassion and God's help.

On the other hand, come to think of it, I hadn't really done anything.

15

It is said that animals don't make mistakes, and that no move they make is awkward. Theoretically, that may be true: they act purely out of instinct, and each animal is exquisitely designed and equipped by nature for whatever its instinct urges it to do. Every healthy bird is a superb athlete, like every mature and healthy dog and cat.

But anyone who has ever owned a dog may have doubts; I have seen full-grown dogs do wonderfully comical things—even pratfalls. And even those supposedly flawless acrobats, the birds, can lose their grip once in a while and do something hysterically funny. I have been corroborated in this by Paul Hoag, the architect, and numerous other eyewitness correspondents.

"Have you ever seen a bird stumble?" Hoag asked me. "Well, I have, twice in my life, and I have to tell you what a pleasure it is."

The first time was in Spokane, when Hoag was a small boy:

"I often watched these big, fat, self-confident robins zoom down on the green grass after a rain and pick up angleworms driven to the surface by the water. I didn't realize how much I envied the robins' self-confidence (which I had in short supply at the time) until right in front of me one of them, just as he touched down for a landing, tripped and fell flat on his face, as we would say."

But Hoag had been telling that story for fifty years, he said, and never come across anyone who had seen the same sort of thing. Then recently he saw it happen again:

"This time it was a finch (an equally cocky breed). Even better, he was not after a worm but just hopping along our deck when his foot slipped into a crack and he fell flat on his face. It was just as satisfying the second time as it was the first."

Henry Manney, another correspondent on this subject, told me of an incident he witnessed back in the early 1950s while on a passenger ferry crossing the strait from Seattle to Vancouver, through clouds of rain and sea gulls.

"The sea gulls were doing their fancy stunting acts in the draft, and one of them came soaring in to make a Rickenbacker landing on the teak rail. Unfortunately, his feet shot out from under him on the newly varnished wet surface, and he landed on his feathered bum on the deck, sitting much as your basic businessman might under the same circumstances—feet out in front with the toes turned up, wings outspread and touching the deck, tail feathers spread out behind. . . ."

Manney suggested that the vile language this

unhappy bird poured out on the laughing passengers and the gallery of his fellows looking down from the rail was proof enough of his embarrassment.

I can't say that I have ever seen a bird stumble, though I have seen them do numerous ridiculous things: fight themselves in shiny hubcaps, fly into windows. These follies are caused by visual illusions, however, and not by a failure of the bird's physical coordination.

But animals sometimes are undone by conditions for which nature has not prepared them. Their skills are unavailing. They trip, they skid, they lose their balance, they tumble. And naturally we crack up because we are relatively awkward creatures, always attempting something nature did not anticipate in her design, and it is gratifying to see our superiors take a fall. It is the old banana-peel psychology.

However, to me the most interesting aspect of these animal accidents is not that they occasionally happen, but that their victims are embarrassed. I have seen animals embarrassed many times, yet embarrassment implies a sense of injured dignity, and a purely instinctive creature is not supposed to be capable of such feelings, is he?

When I was a small boy we had for a time (until he was hit by a car) a stray pit bull named Buddy that waited every day for my sister to come home on the streetcar. She would drop off at the corner and he would run down the street to meet her. One time, however, he ran down the street to meet a girl alighting from the streetcar only to discover that she was not my sister, at which moment he skidded to a stop, looking quite chagrined, and slunk back to the house, tail between his legs, head down, eyes averted, and ears flat, to soften our laughter. That was an embarrassed dog.

My Airedale was perhaps not as smart as that pit bull was, and perhaps not as capable of such deep embarrassment, but he was much more often worthy of it, especially when I let him into the kitchen in the evening, after the kitchen floor had been waxed. His performance was simply hilarious, and my grandchildren begged to see it.

Loving company and expecting to be fed, he of course leaped over the threshold into the kitchen. But the waxed floor gave him no traction, and he would skid across it like a comic skater across the ice. Then all four feet would go out and he would land on his side with a thump. His heroic efforts to regain his feet were even more agonizing than his original downfall, and we would collapse in hysterical, helpless, whimpering laughter.

Once he had righted himself, which he managed to do finally by placing his chin against the floor and raising himself one quarter at a time, something like a camel, his embarrassment was so poignant that we would try to stifle our laughter and pretend we hadn't noticed.

R. A. Schermerhorn told about a man and woman who used to live next door to him. They had a white terrier that was allowed to run upstairs every morning and jump on their bed. "But one morning they started spring housecleaning early by removing their mattress and springs for a little sunning. I happened to be there with the husband when the terrier followed his regular routine by leaping on the bed. There was nothing there but empty space—and he landed on the hardwood floor with a mighty bump. With a look of offended dignity mixed with rage, he raced out and back down the stairs. I still crack up when I remember his embarrassment."

Come to think of it, though, I've never seen an embarrassed cat.

16

Pugsley had no more than rendered the poodles' doghouse uninhabitable than the winter rains came.

We had hoped that before it rained we could get new doghouses built—one for the poodles and one for Pugs himself. Beau and Jolie had proved quite compatible as posslqs (persons of opposite sex sharing living quarters). But it had been a dry fall, and when the rain did come in late December, it was a cloudburst and it caught us by surprise. In minutes the yard was drenched.

To make things worse, workmen had been excavating under the house to firm up our foundation against earthquakes, and the dog yard was covered temporarily by a great pile of dirt. After a few minutes of the downpour it was a quagmire.

The storm woke me up. I got out of bed and went to the back door in my pajamas and slippers to let the dogs in and they bounded toward me. They had been frolicking in the mud. Before they could slip through the door I stepped out and shut it behind me and ran down to the garage and opened the door so they could take shelter in it. In their muddied state they would have ruined the house.

I shut the garage door and ran back to the house to get out of the rain, but I hadn't released the night latch. I hammered on the door until Denny appeared in the window in her robe, shaking her head.

All I needed, I thought, was for Dalton to look out his window at the storm and see me locked out of my own house in the rain in my pajamas.

When the rain stopped I went down to the garage to see how the dogs were getting along. I was dismayed. Pugsley had gotten into a large carton of clothes and remnants Denny had put aside for the Goodwill, and had festooned the garage with its contents. Old dresses and stockings and swimsuits hung from stored or discarded objects like banners.

I turned the dogs out into the yard. They could shelter under the back porch, which they often did to get out of the sun. Surely they had enough sense to get out of the rain.

Later we heard mysterious thumpings under the house and discovered that the workmen had left the crawl hole open. The dogs had moved in. I saw no harm in it. It was a temporary solution to our common problem.

Two days later our television screen began to snow. When Curt came over to build the new doghouses, he crawled under the house to see if something had happened to the cable. He emerged with a mangled section of it.

"Here's what's wrong with your TV," he said. "Your cable's been chewed through."

"Pugs," I said.

I had called Theta, the cable company, and wondered what to tell their man when he showed up. It might be just as well, I thought, not to tell him the damage was done by our own dog. Maybe that wouldn't come under the guarantee. But I am never dishonest with repairmen.

The next morning his van pulled up and he stepped out in fresh-laundered blue coveralls.

"Look's like something chewed up the cable," I said. It was true enough.

He nodded. "Little animals get under the house."

"Lots of wildlife on this hill," I threw in, which was also true.

"No problem. We'll put you in a new cable."

Suddenly the Airedale galloped up. He stood on his hind legs and placed muddy paws on the cable man's spotless uniform.

"Down!" I shouted, and grabbed him away, but the damage was done. The cable man shrugged. He was used to friendly dogs, too.

I thought it had been sensible of me to let the dogs stay under the house while it was raining—at least it served in the emergency; but not everyone agreed. I received a number of eloquent dissents.

"I cannot describe," one woman told me, "the revulsion and contempt that rise in my gorge."

"How could you," said a Mrs. White, "turn them out in the rainy cold weather of Christmas weekend?"

The most alarming thought came from a Mrs. Greene, who said her husband let their springer spaniels stay under their house and later the house got fleas. They had to call an exterminator, who told them the dirt under a house is a good breeding ground for fleas.

Whatever my culpability, my punishment was abundant. Not only had Pugsley knocked out our television picture, he had also dug a hole under our foundation. I felt like a captain whose ship had survived a communications system knockout above decks, only to be holed by a torpedo under the waterline. We were so busy on damage control topside we hadn't even seen it coming.

Getting the doghouses built took time because Curt was studying for a master's in environmental geography at UCLA and had to divide his time between his studies and the doghouses. As far as I know, ours were the only doghouses ever built by a graduate student in environmental geology.

The first house finished was to have been for the Airedale, although some people said we should have built for the poodles first, since the poodle is commonly thought to be more delicate than the Airedale, but that is not true. The poodle was developed in Bavaria as a sheepdog (I have an idea the white poodle was bred for white sheep, the black poodle for black sheep, and the gray for gray sheep, but I can't confirm this) and the breed is able to withstand nasty weather better than most dogs.

Curt built the first house about three feet square and two feet high, with a roof that could be lifted off for easy cleaning. When it was finished we lifted off the roof, dropped Pugsley in, and then put the roof back in place. He stood up, dislodged the roof, and walked out, as if to say, "Sorry, I'm afraid it isn't quite what I had in mind."

So the poodles got the first house after all. As soon as they moved in, Pugsley began chewing at the corners of the top, and Curt had to edge it with aluminum stripping. It didn't take Pugsley long to test the metal, but he couldn't bite through it, so that test was passed.

That left us nothing to worry about but the hole under the foundation and the gestation period of the flea.

After the second doghouse was finished we prayed for another rain so we could find out if the Airedale would figure out what it was for and take shelter in it.

The poodles adapted quickly to their house, not from intelligence so much as from anxiety. They would take cover in it from every noise and shadow. Pugsley tried for a time to follow them in, either for playful harassment or for company, but Curt had deliberately made the door too small for him after the poodles moved in, or thought he had. His own house the Airedale ignored, night and day.

Then one day Pugsley learned how to remove the crawl hole cover and took to living under our house again. I built a dry wall of cement blocks in front of the hole but he knocked it down. Finally, as a stopgap, we moved the poodle house from its place beside the Airedale house and set it in front of the crawl hole. It was too heavy for the Airedale to move.

This kept him out from under the house, but the poodles couldn't relate to their house in its new location and moved into the Airedale house. It wouldn't matter much until it rained. Then I would have to get the poodles out of the Airedale house and get the Airedale in, and get the poodles into their own house.

That's the way it was when the next rain came. When it started coming down hard, I looked out the kitchen window to see what was happening. The poodles were out of sight. They were obviously in Pugsley's house. Pugsley was standing in the rain like a horse.

I slipped into a jacket and stuck my feet in some old shoes and went outside and shouted into the Airedale doghouse, "Out! Get into your own house!" I got to my knees to see if I could reach in and pull the poodles out. The Airedale jumped on my back.

I lifted the Airedale house by one corner and shook the poodles out. They skulked away. I caught the Airedale by his collar and put his head in his house and wrestled him in. It wasn't easy. He was strong as a bear and wet as a walrus.

When I got him in I went after the poodles. They were hiding in the hibiscus. The yard was mud. In two steps it sucked my shoes off. I got one of the poodles under each arm and carried them to their house in my stocking feet. I shoved one in, and was trying to shove the other in left-handed, when the Airedale jumped on my back again.

At this point I began to see that action wasn't going to work. I remembered what Julie Macdonald, the animal sculptor, had said. "Animals never make mistakes. People make mistakes." Animals are not as likely to do harmful things to themselves as people are. An animal usually acts out of instinct, in its own best interest.

Maybe Pugsley was heeding some atavistic impulse that was beyond my understanding. Perhaps it was only that he could not bear to be confined when it was raining. Maybe his ears were too sensitive to tolerate the sound of raindrops on the roof. Maybe there was something in the rain that touched something deep in his genetic memory.

For the time being, I solved the problem by opening the back door to the garage. I could have moved the poodle house away from the crawl hole and let the Airedale live under the house, but I didn't want him to chew up the television cable again. And I didn't want fleas.

I found my shoes and stepped into them and worked them out of the mud and started back into the house, but Denny was at the door looking out at me.

"You'd better go round to the front porch," she shouted, "and take your shoes off!"

I was taking my shoes off on the porch when the postman chattered up in his jeep. He tromped up on the porch in his boots and slicker.

"You get locked out, Jack?"

"It's my Airedale," I explained. "He doesn't have enough sense to come in out of the rain."

"I thought Airedales were smarter than people."

"Not this one."

"Well, here's your mail."

The Airedale not only spent the night in the garage, as I had hoped, but chewed up a year's back issues of the *Intellectual Digest*. I was pleased, at least, that his taste had improved since he had chewed the television cable.

My handling of this emergency brought more indignant reproaches, but several people, especially those who had had some experience with Airedales, were sympathetic, complaining only that I had erred in trying to make the Airedale stay in the doghouse.

One correspondent said she had an Airedale that not only liked rain, but dug holes in the yard when it rained so they would fill up with rainwater and she could take a bath. "By the way," the woman added, "we have a lovely large doghouse she has never set a paw in."

Another woman not only pointed out that Airedales are admirably equipped for wet weather, but she also sent a quote from a dog book noting that the Airedale is a descendant of the otter-hound . . . "from which he takes his all-weather coat and his hearty love of water."

Even more enlightenment on this point was offered by one Harriet Bemus. "Obviously," she wrote, "you have made no effort to understand his heritage, nor do you realize that his behavior is that of a true blueblooded Airedale. . . .

"My home was in Calderdale, near Wuthering Heights, of the Brontës, and adjacent to Airedale. The River Calder and the River Aire run into the River Ouse. Some years there it rains almost every day, and if ever the grass becomes brown, through lack of rain, it's a national disaster. So naturally your dog, developed as an outside dog, prefers rain to sun, and only comes in for worthwhile projects such as demolishing TV cables and digesting intellectual material. . . ."

Fleetwood Pugsley never did learn to stay in his doghouse when it rained. Often, over the years, I would see him standing on the patio a few feet from the open door of his house, feet planted wide, head down. It was the stance of a bull that has been tormented by the picadors and suddenly knows he is alone with death. The stance was similar, but not the spirit. Pugs looked exultant.

I like the rain too. It's not impossible, come to think of it, that my own forebears came from Airedale. Perhaps I, too, like Pugsley, when the weather is foul, dream of a green land where the River Calder and the River Aire run into the River Ouse.

17

Since we live near the top of the hill, above the flooding streets and gutters, when it rains odd creatures seek out our door. They are the dispossessed, the strayed, the drenched.

In one memorable storm we received, among other souls, a gray cat, an Irish setter, a tarantula, some kind of large brown arachnid and a man in a Volkswagen who was lost.

Denny found the arachnid in the sunroom. We didn't know how he got in.

"Come here," she called calmly. "We have a visitor."

It was a very large bug. He was a rich golden brown, like a new football, with darker stripes. He had a trapped, nervous look.

"We'll have to put him out," I decided. "You get a milk carton and catch him. I'll look him up in the encyclopedia."

"Why don't I look him up?"

"You wouldn't know where to begin," I explained. "I've had more experience with research."

I went into the den to look up the bug while she got a milk carton and went after him.

I couldn't find him under Insects. It occurred to me that maybe he wasn't actually an insect. Not everything we call an insect is a true insect. I looked up spiders, although he looked more like a scorpion than a spider. I quickly learned that spiders and scorpions are related, both being of the class Arachnida.

"He's related to the scorpion," I called out, thinking it might help her if she knew what kind of an animal she was dealing with.

She came in with the milk carton. "I'm not catching any scorpions," she said.

"Most arachnids are harmless," I told her. "Did you notice if he had any fangs at the end of his mandibles?"

There was a meowing at the front door. It was the cat, wet and gaunt. We took it into the kitchen and were giving it a bowl of milk when the doorbell rang.

It was the man in the Volkswagen. He said he had been lost for an hour, and was desperate. His clothes were soaked and his boots were muddy. I got out our map book and sent him on his way with new hope.

By that time the bug had vanished.

We found the tarantula that night at the front door. We wondered if he could have fallen off the boots of the Volkswagen man. He was small for a tarantula, but hairy enough.

"You catch him," Denny said. "I'll look him up. She went into the den and shut the door.

I went into the kitchen to get the broom. I didn't have to wait for her to look him up. I knew a tarantula when I saw one. I swept him into the bushes.

The setter was sitting on the doormat the next morning. We took to each other instantly. I always get along with setters. We have the same nervous system—friendly enough, but a little flakey. I put the cat out and the dog in. I kept him all night, but as soon as he dried out I opened the door for him and he trotted off.

So the dog and the tarantula were gone—back, I hoped, to wherever they had come from. As far as we knew, the man in the Volkswagen might still be lost.

For days, though, we had an uneasy feeling that the arachnid had moved in.

As a student of animal psychology, I drove over to the zoo the next Sunday morning to see how animals behave in the rain. For one thing, I wanted to see if there were any clues in nature to my Airedale's habit of standing out in the rain instead of taking shelter in his doghouse.

I had the zoo to myself. It was raining hard and not another visitor was in sight when I bought my ticket and headed up the road through the dripping vegetation.

I soon found myself looking into a pen at a pair of double-wattled cassowaries. They were sitting on the ground under a willow tree, looking mean but unruffled. Raindrops bounced off their backs. For sheer malice of expression, no animal can match the cassowary, except perhaps its cousin the ostrich. They are dangerous birds. The male is monogamous, which is nothing less than prudent of him, considering that the female is larger, and is armed with powerful kicking legs whose inner toes have long sharp nails.

There was a row of birds on the fence, mostly sparrows and blackbirds. In a moment the female cassowary got up and padded over to examine me. The birds scattered but I held my ground. We glared at each other in mutual distaste. I wavered at last and skulked away.

The wombats and wallabies were out of sight. That didn't prove anything. An Australian marsupial is a long way from an Airedale. There were two kea parrots in a tree with their heads tucked under their wings, but of course that's a trick a dog can't do.

I walked on to North America, still quite alone, the only human being in a world of beasts. I soon discovered that this made me an object of curiosity. On an ordinary day, when the place was crowded, the animals wouldn't have given me a glance. Today they found me unique. They interrupted their philosophical reflections, or whatever engaged them, to give me at least a cursory appraisal, and most of them trotted over for a visit.

Even the coyote, the wariest of creatures, loped over to look me straight in the eye. His own eyes were green and beautiful and exquisitely alert. I made the slightest of moves, a flutter of the hands, and he darted off with a thrilling lightness and grace.

Farther on, a sable antelope came over to the fence and wagged his tail. I don't know if tail wagging is typical behavior in a ruminant; but make no mistake, this one did it.

The gorillas were sitting under a canopy. Evidently they preferred staying out of the rain. But then the gorilla is more nearly human than an Airedale. All four of them scowled at me with those astonishingly human faces, and suddenly the largest one reached the glass in two long hops and slapped the iron bars a mighty whack. I was so startled my feet turned numb.

Having got my attention, he then began skating over the rain-slick concrete, exactly like one of the clowns in the Ice Follies—dipping, pirouetting, gliding, skating backward. It was all for me and I applauded.

The Canadian lynx had taken shelter. She was curled up cat-like under a wooden shelf, just out of the rain. But cats are paranoid about water, and their behavior can hardly be regarded as normal.

I found the timber wolves out in the rain and obviously liking it. They seemed less restless than usual. They not only looked at me with something akin to amiability, but the male, I swear it, waved his tail at me like the sable antelope.

When I got home I was soaked to the knee. But it had been a good adventure. For an hour I had been alone with the animals; Tarzan in a raincoat. I poured myself a glass of sherry and sat down to assess my findings. My tentative conclusion was that people are foolishly afraid of the rain, but animals aren't—except wombats, wallabies and cats.

For many years, psychiatrists have been experimenting with animals to find out what causes them to become emotionally depressed. Doctors hope that by discovering the secrets of pathological melancholy in animals they may learn something about this common malaise in people, and perhaps how to alleviate it. Two psychiatrists who made one study concentrated on lovebirds and dogs. They cited the case of a lovebird that slowly faded and died of melancholy after it was put in a cage with two other lovebirds that had formed "a lasting bond."

There certainly should be no mystery about a case like that. Anyone who has ever had to spend any time with a couple of honeymooners can sympathize with this bird. The endless cooing, mooning and feather ruffling between a pair of lovebirds in the clutch of a lasting bond would drive most birds beyond melancholy and into violence, or heavy drinking. It's lucky this *ménage à trois* didn't end up with three dead birds, instead of one.

As usual, poets are a step ahead of psychiatrists when it comes to understanding love and loneliness, sexual bondage and melancholy.

> *She's only a bird in a gilded cage,*
> *A pitiful sight to see . . .*

The poet who penned that poignant ballad anticipated the present scientific inquiry into similarities of human and animal depression by nearly a century.

We have all seen melancholy in animals. One day at the zoo I saw an orangutan sink into a funk. He had been sporting with his playmates. Suddenly he stopped and looked deep into my eyes. Then he swung over to the wall of the pen and slipped down into a small dejected heap. He looked out at the people with exactly the expression of the creature in that old cartoon which gained such a wide circulation among soldiers in World War II. It showed some kind of anthropoid, probably a corporal, sitting in the same kind of funk in a cage. The caption said, "People are no damn good."

The orangutan at the zoo obviously had been struck by this same insight.

The psychiatrists will find that what causes dogs, birds and monkeys to be melancholy is the same thing that causes people to be melancholy. Life.

18

Though my wife usually fed the cats in the morning before leaving the house for work, it was my chore to put them out. I sometimes wondered if that was why they favored her, as the poodles did, while regarding me with a certain distrust (an explanation which now seems too simple).

Gato rarely protested. I simply opened the door and said, "Out," and she walked out, not so fast, however, as to part with her style and dignity. Mozart, on the other hand, was crafty. She could sense when I was about to put her out, and would often quietly disappear. She showed remarkable ingenuity in finding places to hide. Never the same place twice in a row, once discovered in it. She hid under beds, in closets, in boxes, in open bureau drawers, and sometimes, with exasperating arrogance (baiting the lion) she would hide under my desk, the place she seemed to know I would be least likely to look.

She once outwitted me for days in a row. I

would look in all the usual places, even getting down on my hands and knees (which I disliked) only to give up, thinking she must have gone out when Denny left. Later she would turn up sacked out innocently on the couch. I simply couldn't figure out her hiding place.

As so often happens in such mysteries, the solution was revealed to me by chance. I was drawing back the floor-length curtains one morning to let the light in through the picture window and saw a paw. She was hiding behind the curtain, at the far end, opposite the pull cord, twelve feet away. Inch by inch the curtain folded back and moved toward me. I never saw the cat. At last the curtain was fully drawn. I got down on my hands and knees and raised the bottom of the curtain off the floor. There she was. We were eyeball-to-eyeball. She hissed. I blinked.

That evening I was trying to tell my French daughter-in-law about this ruse. "So that was it," I said. "She was hiding under the curtain, and whenever I opened it, she crept along with it, as it moved, and hid in the fold at the end."

"Mr. Smith," my daughter-in-law asked, conceding me, as always, the courtesy title my position called for in her French provincial bringing up, "why do you have two cats when they give you so much trouble?"

"Well," I explained, "I'm not responsible for the cats. Mozart there, she belongs to your husband, and Gato belongs to his brother."

"I do not understand."

"Do you understand baseball?"

"Oui. Yes, certainly. My husband has learn me."

I explained that the cats had been stray kittens, and that our two sons, when they were boys, had taken them in. Doug, her husband, had found the black cat outside a church in the neighborhood, and Curt had found the calico in a motel in Ensenada and smuggled her across the border in our car. Then, of course, the boys had grown up and gone to college and got married and started their own families and the cats had grown up too, as they do, and stayed behind.

"So, technically," I said, "the cats belong to the boys."

"I do not understand."

"It's like in baseball. One pitcher lets a man get on base, and then leaves the game. And then another pitcher comes in and lets a man get on base, and he leaves the game. Then the third pitcher comes in. Even though the first pitcher is actually responsible for the first runner, and the second pitcher is responsible for the second runner, the third pitcher inherits them both. They're his problem. You see?"

Our eyes met for a long moment. "The pitcher," she said at last, "he is the one with the stick?"

"Mon Dieu!" I sighed.

"I know there is a man with a stick, and a man with a glove and a man with the ball."

Sometimes my daughter-in-law reminds me very much of Mozart.

With my hands full of cats at home, I wouldn't have thought I could work up the slightest concern for

a kitten lost in the wilderness of New York City—
a kitten I had never seen and would never see.

It happened to be the summer of New York
City's discontent, but my wife and I, on one of our
rare visits, enjoyed ourselves on its sidewalks, exhilarated by its vitality, its infinite variety, its sense
of unlimited possibilities.

The city was then sliding toward the abyss of
bankruptcy, and the men who had got it there were
working through the night, trying to get it out. The
whole city was playing it with the tremulous bra-
vado of a Broadway show on its last night before
closing because its angels had run out of money.

A few days after I got home, as I read the horror stories of mass layoffs, strikes, fear, anguish and
decay, it occurred to me that I may have had the
only good news to come out of New York City in
two weeks.

The day we were walking on Broadway in lower
Manhattan near City Hall park, the very place
where laid-off policemen had been demonstrating
against the city and clashing with their former
comrades, I happened to see a small paper notice
pasted to a streetcorner post, the kind of hand-
printed note we see all over the residential neighborhoods of Los Angeles, advertising for the return of lost dogs or lost cats or lost whatevers.

"LOST: Female white cat," this one said. "Blind
in one eye. Answers to the name of Kevin."

There was a phone number, and for some reason I took it down. It seemed so improbable, so
refreshing, that anyone could be optimistic enough
to post such a notice there in the heart of down-

town Manhattan, a few steps from the Woolworth Building and the Brooklyn Bridge, on a street corner shadowed by skyscrapers, clogged with vehicles and pedestrians, and filled with the din of New York City life.

After we got home, a week or so went by before I came to that small entry in my notebook. I wondered if Kevin had ever been found or come home. I put it out of my mind. What difference did it make? There were 10,000 lost cats in Los Angeles. Why worry about a lost cat in New York? It was another week before I telephoned. I had to find out.

I dialed the New York number, wondering how to explain myself if anyone answered.

"Hello?" It was the voice of a young woman, judging from its timbre and buoyancy, and it had a touch of British in it.

"This is Jack Smith," I began, realizing that this would tell her absolutely nothing.

"I beg your pardon?"

"I live in Los Angeles."

"Yes?"

I rather liked her. She seemed only slightly surprised and puzzled that someone named Jack Smith should be phoning her from Los Angeles. Her voice reflected more curiosity than caution.

"I was in New York a week or two ago," I went on, "and I saw your note about your cat. Kevin."

"Oh. I see. Yes."

"And I just wondered if you'd found it."

"No, we haven't found her yet."

"That's too bad," I said lamely.

"Oh, it's terrible, because she's been gone now for two weeks."

"I doubt," I said, "that in New York City, you're likely to find her. Don't you?"

"Yes, I do. I doubt it. But I know that she's a pretty smart animal, and I think she'd come back, if she got out. That is, I imagine somebody's picked her up and taken her home. She's so beautiful, you know. She's a tiny white cat, and she's really pretty.

"We've had a few calls," she went on, "but they haven't been our cat. But we still have hopes we'll find her. We're still advertising in the *Times* and the *Voice*."

"Well, I hope you find her."

"Thank you very much for calling," she said. "You must be a cat lover."

That gave me pause. "I admire cats." I said. "I'm just a newspaper writer, and it seemed like a good story. By the way, you sound English."

"No, I'm Australian, actually. That's twelve thousand miles away from England. Don't worry. You can put that in."

I wondered what had brought her all the way from Australia to New York City.

"I'm a painter," she said, "and this is where it's all going on, apparently."

She said her name was Wendy Frost, and she would let me know if Kevin turned up. When I hung up I realized that I hadn't asked her how the cat happened to be blind in one eye, and how a female got a name like Kevin.

I felt a surge of envy for Wendy Frost, as well as admiration; it was naive but wonderful to believe that a small half-blind cat could be found in a teeming metropolis that was on the brink of chaos.

Then I didn't think about it again until days later when the young woman who takes my phone calls at the office said I'd had a call from New York, from a Ms. Frost.

"Oh?" I said. "What was the message?"

"She said she found her cat."

I didn't phone to ask her how she'd found it. It would have been good enough for O. Henry that she had. It was good enough for me.

19

For years I have been widely regarded as an expert on birds. I find that amusing, but also embarrassing. I hardly know one bird from another, and that reputation is based on a single chance sighting years ago in my backyard—a sighting which, ironically, made me the laughing stock of the bird-watching establishment.

While I do take satisfaction in being vindicated in that instance, the reputation that has derived from it is without further foundation.

I have tried many times to disabuse those who innocently believe the myth. I have tried everything. Honesty. Confession. Self-deprecation. Humor. But once you get a reputation for something, good or bad, you can't get rid of it.

Not a week goes by that I don't get letters or phone calls beginning, "I know you're a bird expert. . . ."

I am reminded of Agnes Allen's Law: "Everything is easier to get into than out of."

Finally, I'm afraid, I'll begin to believe it myself.

I got myself into this predicament in the first place. It was many years ago, but as I remember it, I had gone outdoors that morning to write an essay about spring. I don't remember whether it was spring, but it was a pleasant day, it seemed like spring, and in Los Angeles you can't really tell what season it is.

The sky was blue, the air was bracing, and everything was fresh and clean. I was trying to get it down in longhand on my yellow legal pad—the color of the flowers, the flight of the birds and dragonflies and butterflies, the texture of it— meanwhile sipping from a mug of coffee. Suddenly a bird flew low over the birdbath, chattering, dipped a wing in the water, and then flew up and out over the yard and down into the canyon out of sight.

I thought that would be a nice touch, put some life in the thing, and I tried to describe the incident. It occurred to me, though, that it would be more vivid if I said what kind of bird it was; in writing, the specific is said to be more forceful and graphic than the general.

But, alas, I didn't know what kind of bird it was. It had been just a common-looking bird, and at that time I hardly knew one bird from another, except for pelicans, penguins, owls, parrots, flamingos— that sort of thing—and one or two that are extinct. But I knew a lot of bird names. They are so vivid and colorful and metaphorical and evocative. The name grackle came to mind. I didn't know what a grackle looked like, but I liked the name, and I knew the grackle was a common bird. Who could say the bird I had seen was not a grackle?

I don't want to give the impression that I am careless of the facts as a reporter; no reporter is more conscientious, but the piece I was trying to write was meant to be fanciful, rich in metaphor and poetic license. And, as I say, it was spring, or seemed like it.

I didn't know it at the time, but the foundation of my reputation was laid the instant that essay was published and read, presumably, by a large number of people, many of them true bird experts.

Among the many letters I received (most of them rather disdainful and supercilious) was one from Ken Stager, then curator of birds at the Museum of Natural History. Like most of the others, Dr. Stager noted that no grackle had ever before been seen west of the Mississippi River, a phrase I was soon to tire of hearing, and as for my sighting, he concluded: "I can't buy it . . ." which I thought admirably succinct for an ornithologist.

What I had seen, Dr. Stager and several others suggested, was a Brewer's blackbird.

I was of course embarrassed. I looked up the grackle and Brewer's blackbird in a bird book. They did look remarkably alike. So much so, in fact, that even an experienced bird-watcher, I thought, might mistake one for the other especially when seen in motion for only a few seconds. If someone could think a Brewer's blackbird was a grackle, why couldn't someone else (even Dr. Stager) mistake a grackle for a Brewer's blackbird?

I decided to stonewall it, though at that time the phrase was not in vogue.

My policy in life has been to believe my own eyes. A great many curious things occur on this earth, but those who first report them are often ignored or scoffed at as fools and troublemakers. The grackle, evidently, had never been seen in this neighborhood, so when one did turn up nobody wanted to believe it. It was human nature.

Having found out how very rare a grackle was in these parts, I naturally had reported my sighting to the Audubon Society, since I am a responsible citizen. It was up to them to determine its authenticity.

With routine courtesy they thanked me, but they didn't put my grackle on their report. The truth was, of course, that they didn't believe it. Their thinking, I suppose, went something like this: Since the grackle had never been known to fly west of the Mississippi River, the grackle I saw was not a grackle.

It was the same kind of thinking one might have expected of a Carib Indian who, finding Christopher Columbus on his beach, would have said he wasn't there because he had never been there before.

I stood by my story. If there were grackles east of the Mississippi, I asked, what was to keep them from flying across it and coming on to Los Angeles? After all, birds do migrate, I pointed out, as no one should know better than the Audubon Society. How did grackles get where they were in the first place?

I suffered months of derision for this heresy. Then one morning I went out to fill the bird feeder and saw another grackle. That is, I saw another large black bird that looked to me like a grackle. I decided it was time to give them something new to think about.

I reported sighting a second grackle in the same location as the first one. I expected the onslaught to be renewed. On the contrary, something completely unexpected happened. My report was not only taken in good humor by a good many people, but the Audubon Society itself was not so quick as it had been the first time to discredit me.

If the Audubon's membership was divided by my second sighting, and some seemed at least to be withholding judgment, this advantage was soon lost when I tested their credibility yet again. I'm afraid this time they thought of me as the little boy who had cried wolf once too often.

What happened was, I sighted an orchard oriole in exactly the same place that I had seen the grackles. This lovely bird, while not unknown in Southern California, had been so rarely seen here that any unconfirmed sighting was met with skepticism, especially when it was reported by an already suspect source.

The sighting was simple luck. I had happened to glance out our window into the garden and saw an unfamiliar-looking bird on a bush. I hadn't the slightest idea what kind of bird it was, but it was a very handsome bird, and I knew I had never seen one like it before.

It was also luck that I had just recently bought my first copy of Roger Peterson's *Field Guide to Western Birds,* and knew exactly where to put my finger on it. Smarting from the grackle affair, I wanted never again to be caught unprepared.

I didn't panic. I didn't dash for the book. If I'd done that, there was a chance that in the interim the bird would fly and I would hurry back to the window, book in hand, to find the bush bare.

So, first I stood quite still in the window and studied the bird intently, stamping every feather on my mind. He was a dark, reddish-brown underneath, going toward black on top, like a man wearing a cutaway over brown overalls. It wasn't a dull or muddy brown, but a high, rich brown like the color of a chestnut racehorse. A fine bird indeed.

Then, as I had feared, he flew away. Quickly I went into the den and got the guide. I thumbed back through the color plates and suddenly his picture leaped out. There was no doubt at all. It might have been a picture I had taken with a Polaroid camera a minute earlier. I had positively seen an orchard oriole.

It was a satisfying experience, seeing a bird I hadn't seen before, and then pinning its identity down so swiftly and surely. But in a moment, as I read on, satisfaction soared to excitement. The orchard oriole, it turned out, was so rare in California as to be classified as "casual." A casual, in Peterson's bag of terms, is rarer than rare: a bird seen once or twice in a decade.

With a glow of self-importance, I phoned Audubon headquarters at once. They would put it out on their hot line, and carloads of bird-watchers would begin arriving at our doorstep within the half hour.

"An orchard oriole?" said the woman who had answered. "I see."

That was the end of it. No carloads of watchers showed up. I doubt that the woman at Audubon ever put it down on the log as a "possible." But the story was leaked. After that, when I was among birders, someone would invariably say something like, "Seen any orchard orioles lately? Heh heh."

They might as well have asked if I'd stopped hallucinating.

At that point, I might have let the grackle affair fade from memory. It had ended at least in a standoff, and if more grackles were sighted in the future, I was sure my unprecedented sighting would be recalled. I would not have to blow my own horn.

Meanwhile I would never mention it again. I couldn't imagine that Darwin would have hung around the pubs of London, trying to cadge drinks by saying, "I'm Chuck Darwin—you know, the fellow who found out that man was descended from the apes."

I couldn't picture myself, either, in a little beer parlor in Los Angeles telling some stranger, "My name is Smith. I was the first person to see a grackle west of the Mississippi River."

Then an event of astounding significance took place.

Denny and I were taking a holiday in New York City when we got word of it by special delivery letter. It was from two men whose names I didn't know—Mike San Miguel and Lewis Hastings of Southern California Edison.

"It came as no surprise," the letter began, "when on May 24 at Furnace Creek Ranch in Death Valley, the first bona fide sighting of the common grackle of California was made. An event as great as this deserves, and did receive, as much fanfare as a full eclipse of the moon."

I was exuberant, despite Hastings' and Miguel's description of this as "the first bona fide sighting" in California (the implication being that my sighting was still not bona fide).

A rather more reasonable interpretation of the Furnace Creek incident came from Harold Lichterman, a Los Angeles attorney: "I thought you would like to know," he said, "that Los Angeles Audubon is reporting what they call 'the first California sighting of a common grackle at Furnace Creek in Death Valley.' I don't know why they have not accepted your previous sightings as authentic, but now you have been vindicated."

So the grackles I had seen were evidently scouts. If so, why had they led their followers to Death Valley (which is not terribly nice in the summer) instead of to Los Angeles, or even San Francisco? Perhaps, I thought, they meant to winter in Death Valley and summer on the coast.

I came home from New York a modest hero. I

could hardly rank myself with Copernicus, Newton and Darwin; and yet, in a sense, I had tasted of the same bitter fruit. Each of us had come across truths that the Establishment hadn't wished to accept—truths that were before their time.

But the sighting at Furnace Creek was followed quickly by the appearance of the broadbilled hummingbird at the Trimmer house not far from ours on Mt. Washington. This bird, as we have seen, had never before been sighted in Los Angeles, and only a handful of times in California.

Then came yet another startling development and another vindication. I heard of it first in a letter from the eminent birder Chuck Bernstein: "Those who scoffed at your sighting of the orchard oriole (almost everyone) scoff no more. Two weeks ago, within sight of your house, a male in fall plumage was verified and photographed at a hummingbird feeder!"

Only then did it begin to occur to the more liberal thinkers of the society that there might be something peculiar about Mt. Washington besides its residents. As Bernstein put it, "Every errant bird in California must have a flight path over that hill!"

It would be dishonest to imply that the Audubon Society rewrote its own records to acknowledge my contribution in the case of the grackle. After all, look how long it took the Church even to reconsider its rejection of Copernicus.

But their attitude toward me changed dramatically. I was invited to attend the next annual banquet of the Los Angeles chapter as its guest of honor. I was made an honorary member, and its president presented me with a framed drawing of a common grackle bearing the legend: California common grackle, *Quiscalus quiscula Smith*. (I assume the Smith was tacked on in jest, but of course if the bird I saw should turn out to have been a slightly different subspecies, I suppose that in time, perhaps posthumously, it might bear my name.)

I hope I will be forgiven for dwelling on this story with what must seem a shameless lack of modesty. Birders are not in general glory seekers, though the field has its peacocks, like any other. On the contrary, they are happiest out in the field and stream, far from the clangor of conflict and publicity. But this may be my last chance to bring all the facts together, for the record.

My euphoria was dampened, though, by the knowledge that the bird whose coming it had been my lot to herald, was not exactly welcome. The fact is that the common grackle is not a nice bird. They are handsome enough, being large and black with bronze or purple backs and a flash of iridescence in the sunlight, but they are greedy crop eaters and ferocious nest robbers. They will even attack other adult birds, piercing their skulls with large, sharp beaks and eating their brains. In Eastern and Midwestern states they often attack in noisy, frightening clouds, darkening the sky, blackening the trees and devastating the earth. Nothing prevails against them but chemical warfare.

Most Southern Californians hadn't even known there was such a bird as the grackle, and thought I had made it up.

They will believe in grackles soon enough, I imagine, when the whole species comes to California and we are up to our ears in grackles. It will be a black day for all of us, and especially for me, if the accursed bird bears my name.

Why couldn't I have sighted a Chinese nightingale?

20

Considering that we live no more than a ten-minute drive from everything in the world that money can buy, my wife is strangely addicted to mail-order shopping. This probably comes from her girlhood in an isolated small town, where she discovered that a three-cent stamp, ten cents and a magazine coupon would in time bring something wonderful to her door.

However she got started, I know that she is hooked the way some women are hooked on candy or gin. There still is something magic in it for her, I suppose, and I myself am not immune to the flutter of surprise and pleasure that comes when the long-awaited package is found on the porch at the end of a frustrating day.

By now we must be on every mailing list there is, some of them, no doubt, of a kind that could bring us to the attention of the FBI. We have long since learned that to do business with one mail-order house is to have one's name peddled to half a dozen others, along with some notes about one's merits as a customer: "Pays fairly promptly. . . . This one will buy anything. . . . Never returns merchandise. . . . " (We would no more return something we had ordered than we'd shoplift.)

As I say, I thought we had already been subjected to every pitch that could be made through the mails, but we found something in our box one day which proved that we had underestimated the ingenuity and reach of the mail-order industry. It was a package addressed to Pugsley and Gato, which happened, of course, to be the names of our dog and cat.

I am disinclined to open other people's mail, even if it's only printed advertising matter, but not to do so in this case would have seemed to be carrying a principle too far. The package was stuffed with merchandising coupons and offers, including one for cat food. "Dreams are wishes," it said. "We all know that. When a cat dreams of little blue cans it's because of what he finds inside. . . . Make your cat's dreams come true with the coupon below."

My mind was relieved on one point at least. The ads were not written as if the authors expected them to be read by the addressees. In a lifetime of observing dogs and cats I am convinced they cannot talk, and they certainly can't read. Consequently, I have no patience with anything that is made to sound as if it had been written by a dog or cat or in contemplation of its being read by one. I also refuse to see a movie in which animals talk, especially mules. (For some reason, I don't mind animals talking in cartoons. Who doesn't love Mickey Mouse, Bugs Bunny and Sylvester?)

The rest of the leaflets and coupons advertised merchandise that would be of little interest to the dog or cat, such as the *Encyclopaedia Britannica*, five-acre ranches in Utah and pantyhose at 99¢ a pair.

What puzzled me about the package was how the people who sent it got our dog and cat's address. We had never given it out.

"I think I know," Denny said. "It was that book with our names in it."

She found it in a drawer full of mail-order literature. It was one of those computerized books for children in which the child's own name, and street, and the names of his pets, are in the text. The idea, I suppose, is that if a child finds himself the hero of a book he is likely to read it. It certainly worked in my case.

Evidently they had got our names from one of those sources that sell such information, but there was some misunderstanding about just who or what we were.

The book was called *My Friend the Giraffe. Your Personal Story by the Magic Computer*. It began:

"Once upon a time, in a place called Los Angeles, there lived a little boy named Jack Smith. . . . One morning, Jack was playing with Denise in front of his home. When he looked up, what do you think he saw walking down the middle of Camino Real? You guessed it. A giraffe! . . . Jack realized that he didn't even know the giraffe's name. It cer-

tainly wasn't Pugsley, because that's his dog's name.
And it couldn't be Gato, because the giraffe didn't
look anything like his cat. . . . "

You can guess what had happened. They had
our names all right, but somehow they thought I
was a child and Denise was either my playmate or
my pet (it wasn't clear).

Anyway, now that Pugs and Gato were on
mailing lists, I had an idea they were going to be
more expensive.

It might have been a bit more attractive if Pugs and
Gato had been offered a line of credit to finance
the merchandise they were being asked to buy.

A woman who owned a Hungarian sheepdog
that had never shown any special wit or business
acumen told me she was surprised one day to learn
that the dog had managed to establish a $1,500 line
of credit with a finance company.

The dog's name was Burford.

"He gives every appearance," said this woman,
Mary Hughes Thompson, "of a lazy, good-for-
nothing beast. He seems to be without ambition or
energy."

That being Burford's character, it was easy to
imagine the Thompson's surprise when he received a letter from Aetna Finance enclosing a
"Gold Certificate" entitling "the homeowner named
herein to a golden opportunity of up to $1,500."
It was made out to G. Burford, serial number
100050000049, same address as the Thompsons.
The letter read:

G. Burford:

Because of your excellent credit record, you may be eligible for up to $1,500. Just bring in the Gold Certificate above. To qualify for this unique offer, simply (1) present your Gold Certificate to an office shown on the back; (2) show positive identification, such as driver's license or birth certificate; (3) provide proof of your present income (a paycheck stub or W-2 form); (4) complete an application.

Use this money for any good purpose—a new stereo system, new furniture or maybe even a down payment on a car. And there's no long wait. You'll be surprised at how fast Aetna puts cash in your hands.

Mrs. Thompson told me she wondered whether my Airedale had received any such offer. "For an animal who wouldn't even learn to bring in the morning *Times*," she said, "I think Burford has some explaining to do, don't you?"

My own concern was not with how Burford managed to get himself in the good graces of Aetna Finance, but how he was going to pass their test and get the money. It seemed rather duplicitous of them to tell Burford he had an excellent credit record, and then ask him to come in and prove it. If they already knew his record was excellent, what more did they want?

Even so, Burford should have had no trouble with most of the requirements. He didn't have a driver's license of course, but if the Thompsons were sure he was a Hungarian sheepdog, then there must have been papers on him, including proof of birth. People insist on calling mongrels all sorts of breeds, but I have never heard of anyone with the nerve to pass one off as a Hungarian sheepdog.

As for proof of his income, the Thompsons needed only to come forward with an affidavit setting forth the monetary value of the services they provided for Burford (food, lodging, medical care, grooming, et cetera). If a Hungarian sheepdog cost as much to keep as an Airedale, he was sure to pass.

He could have signed the application with a paw print. I believe the files of Hollywood movie studios are full of contracts signed in this way. A paw print is just as legal as an illiterate person's X, as long as it is properly witnessed.

For a day or two the Thompsons took Burford's windfall as a joke. Obviously it was only one of those computer errors that everyone encounters. And they thought that even if Burford could go to court and force the finance company to make good on its offer, what would he do with the $1,500? He already had an adequate home, and he wouldn't be wanting a car or a stereo system. They didn't forget that he was only a dog.

Then came a development that gave the Thompsons further pause. It was yet another letter, and it began:

"Dear Mrs. Burford . . ."

Mrs. Burford indeed! They knew nothing of any Mrs. Burford, and if Burford was living a double life, they had never suspected it.

The letter was from the National Board of Sweepstakes Review, Cleveland, Ohio, and advised Mrs. Burford that she had won either a Honda moped motor bike, 1,000 gallons of gasoline, a Sony giant screen TV, a 35 mm camera, a new Mustang, a Polavision camera, a smokeless electric barbecue grill, a year's college tuition, or their equivalents in cash . . . if she met the qualifying conditions on the back of the special notice.

The Thompsons were quickly disenchanted, though, when they read the conditions. First, it said, "You or your husband must be over 21 and gainfully employed. Both you and your husband must be present to complete a brief but courteous presentation of Sweetwater Condoshare. . . . "

So that was it. Some kind of real estate promotion. Even if there had been a Mrs. Burford, and she and Burford were married, she wouldn't very likely be 21 years old, and Burford certainly wasn't. So there went the Honda, or that year in college or whichever of the gifts might most have appealed to Mr. and Mrs. Burford.

What I'd like to know is whether Burford and his mate, assuming he did have a secret mate, could have sued the National Board of Sweepstakes Review for excluding unmarried dogs from their offer. It seems to me that an unmarried dog is as entitled to the full protection of the law as a married dog. And I'd like to know why Mrs. Burford had to be married to receive her gift. Isn't that discrimination against the unmarried female?

No wonder they want the ERA.

21

Sometimes it seemed as if Fleetwood Pugsley's only aim in life was to escape our yard. I sympathized with him. He didn't like being fenced in any more than I would, I suppose, but of course we couldn't let him out. Not only is it against the law to let a dog run loose, but it is also a good way to get him poisoned or killed by a car, or to get yourself hauled before the police court for violating the leash ordinance.

Keeping him in required constant vigilance. One week he got out three times, which was a record. However, we began to learn his tactics and developed some countertactics of our own.

He had a routine. When I came home at the end of the day and let him into the house through a backyard door, the first thing he did was make the rounds, checking every door, hoping he would find one open to the street. All doors being secure, he kept an ear tuned for Denny's car engine.

He knew the moment she turned the corner, and waited at the front door ready to make his break—ears up, every sinew taut.

He sometimes made it. She would set her groceries down on the porch and search her key ring for the house key. She would open the door. The dog would dart out, knocking over the groceries. In my den I would hear her cry of dismay and know she'd done it again—or he'd done it again, depending on how you looked at it.

This would activate Phase Two. Denny would run down the street after the dog and I would follow in the car. When she caught him I would drive him home. I suppose I could have chased him on foot myself and let her drive the car, but you have to have a plan and stick to it.

One time he got out through an open gate when we weren't home, and a neighbor caught him for us. "It wasn't easy," he said. "That's a hard dog to catch."

That was an understatement. The instant he cleared the gate he was gone. He ran full out, down the hill, into a yard here, after a cat there, so exuberant he couldn't finish one project before he was into the next. He utterly ignored calls of "Here, Pugs, here fellow," no matter how sternly or affectionately they were put.

Another time that he got out my wife and I caught him with a splendidly coordinated effort, on which our regular drill was based. Running like a gazelle, she followed him into a yard from which, Pugsley discovered too late, there was no escape except past the arms of his mistress. With extraordinary skill and courage, I thought, she tackled him, and just at that moment I rolled up in the car. Perfect teamwork.

The next time he got out, though, I was alone. The gas man had left the gate ajar when he came in to read the meter. "Sir," I heard him call. "Your dog got out."

In a moment I saw Pugs racing up the hill in pursuit of a shaggy brown dog. He ran by me without a sidelong glance. He was giving me the same old treatment—pretending he didn't see me. Now and then the brown dog would turn and take a stand, and the Airedale would bounce around him, barking amiably.

It was hopeless, I thought. And then I noticed something. The brown dog had thrown me a glance. It was an SOS. Perhaps he saw in me an ally. Fleetwood Pugsley, I knew, would never respond to my call. But maybe this dog would. He could be my Judas goat.

"Here fellow," I called, whistling and clapping my hands and trying to make my voice sound sweet and trustworthy. The brown dog headed my way; hesitantly at first, then swiftly as he heard the Airedale's breath behind him. As he neared me he slowed down and crept up to my hands. At that instant the Airedale pounded up and crashed into us. I grabbed him.

Pugsley knew the game was up. He was docile under my hand, and went back through his gate without a protest. I felt gratified. Where my wife had used brute force, I had used wile. A human being can't outrun a dog, so he or she must apply the human animal's superior intelligence.

It happened that Curt and Gail were coming by that morning to pick Pugs up. They were driving down to the house in Baja and wanted to take him along. I had just gotten him back in the yard when they drove up. Curt seemed a bit dubious as he took Pugs on the leash and led him to the car.

"Sure you want him?" I asked.

"It isn't me," he said. "It's Gail."

"If there are many people down there," I told Curt, "he'll follow somebody away. He loves people, and he's hell to catch."

"Gail can catch him," Curt said.

The men in my family have always had the good sense to marry women who are fleet of foot.

The dog law we have observed with such vigilance and energy is the one most commonly flouted on Mt. Washington. Our place is on a three-point corner on one of Mt. Washington's main streets. It is a thoroughfare not only for residents driving down the hill to work or up the hill toward home, but also for their dogs. We have a continual parade of miscellaneous sizes and genetic mixtures. They come in singles, mismated pairs or ragtag little packs, like circus dogs.

I would be troubled by conflicting emotions as I watched this daily promenade and heard my own dog barking and whining in frustration in his pen when they nosed up against the fence. I knew his blood was racing with the urge to be out and running with the others.

Any momentary breakdown in security and he was out—zip. I remember one morning when I was talking to someone at the front door and Denny opened the back door in the kitchen. Pugsley was in through the back door and through the house and out the front door, past me and our visitor, before either Denny or I could even shout for him to stop, which he wouldn't have done, anyway.

It isn't that we begrudged him a few minutes of freedom, but once he was out he was gone for hours, and he ranged wide. Everyone knew him. Everyone liked him.

Sometimes neighbors phoned and said they had our dog, or had just seen him trotting down their street. Sometimes they brought him back, holding him by the collar. They were always sweaty and breathless, and looked at me with dark reproach.

Sometimes Denny would go after him in the car, and sometimes he would hop into it when she found him, but more often he wouldn't. Instead of working on our drill for catching him, we concentrated on security, and he only got out if someone (rarely one of us) opened a gate and shut it carelessly, so it didn't latch.

I thought that was what had happened one day when Denny was out on the front porch watering her plants and I was in my study and heard her give that peace-shattering alarm, "Pugs is out!"

"You must have left the gate unlatched," I shouted.

"No I didn't. I haven't been near it."

"Then it's a mystery," I said, not believing it was a mystery at all. She had to be the guilty one.

She didn't answer, and I realized she had gone after him. Five minutes later she was back. I could hear her struggling up the steps huffing from her exertions and remonstrating with the dog.

"I got him," she said between puffs.

She dragged him through the house and out the back door. In a minute she was back in the house, looking baffled.

"Pugs wasn't out after all," she said in a curious sort of voice, as if she had just had a close encounter of the third kind. "He was in the backyard all the time."

I got up and went into the living room where she stood holding an Airedale by his collar. Only it wasn't the right kind of collar. And suddenly I knew it wasn't the right Airedale, either. He was cleaner than Pugsley, for one thing, and trimmer. We looked each other in the eye and both of us knew we were meeting for the first time. He looked as bewildered as my wife.

"That isn't Pugs," I said.

"Then who is it?" she asked helplessly.

"I've never seen him before," I said.

I'm sorry to say that in our embarrassment and confusion we let the dog loose instead of checking his tag and calling his owners, as they might have done for us. We never saw him again, and I like to think he got home safely and his owners were more careful after that.

But it amused me to wonder what the poor fellow thought when a strange madwoman chased him down cooing "Here, Pugs, here, Pugsie," and grabbed him by the collar and dragged him up the hill and into a strange house.

He must have admired her chutzpah, if nothing else.

Since the location of our house makes it an observation post on this canine Piccadilly Circus, the neighbors naturally count on us to keep a lookout for their dogs too.

One night years ago, a man named Johnson telephoned from his place at the top of the hill and wanted to know if I'd seen his Samoyed. For a second I thought he must be talking about one of those Japanese sports cars. They seem to come out with a new one every month.

"It's a female," he said. "White."

"Oh, a Samoyed," I said. "No, I haven't. But I'll keep an eye peeled."

"It's a female," he repeated.

"OK," I said. "I'll watch for it. Let you know."

I got out my instant dog computer and looked up Samoyed. The computer is one of those ingenious cardboard devices so contrived that when you move an arrow to the dog you have in mind, all the facts about it appear in a window. I keep it handy to help me identify interesting strays and to look up my neighbors' dogs when they call me to watch for a miniature Schnauzer or a Japanese spaniel or whatever.

Samoyed was listed in the working dog group. The computer said it would weigh thirty-five to fifty-five pounds, the coat being pure white or biscuit-cream in color; the texture long, harsh and straight. I also looked it up in Webster's, to make sure. "Any of a Siberian breed of medium-sized deep-chested white or cream-colored arctic dogs," it said.

I decided that if I did see the dog I would simply phone Johnson, instead of investigating. I didn't intend to get close enough to a medium-sized deep-chested Siberian arctic working dog to find out whether it was a male or a female.

Oddly, that same afternoon as Denny and I were driving up the hill we met our neighbors the Walletts driving down. Just as we passed I realized they had a big white dog in the back seat.

"D'you think Wallett would steal a dog?" I asked Denny.

"What are you talking about?"

"Oh, nothing. I suppose it's just a coincidence."

All the same, I couldn't get it out of my mind. A day or two later I decided it wouldn't hurt to check it out. I phoned Wallett. He lives just across the canyon and I could have walked over, but I didn't want to be that direct.

"Bill," I said, "you know that big white dog I saw you with?"

"Oh, yes," he said. "Sam."

"What kind of a dog is that?"

"Why Sam's a Belgian shepherd," he said. "Why?"

"Oh, I just wondered," I said. "I'm interested in dog identification, you know. It's sort of a hobby. When birds are out of season."

I wasn't sure whether the Wallett dog actually was a Belgian shepherd or whether that was just quick thinking on Wallett's part. I ran through the computer and found a breed called Belgian sheepdog. Weight, forty-five to sixty pounds, it said. That seemed about right. Color, black. Black? Then Wallett's dog was no more a Belgian sheepdog than my Airedale was, unless of course it was an albino. Also, there was the fact that its name was Sam. But I once knew a girl named Sam, so it could still be a female.

The next night I came home to find a third dog in our dog yard. Beau, who had developed a nervous disorder, was no longer with us, but we still had Jolie and the Airedale, which was one dog too many and sometimes, I thought, two dogs too many. The last thing we needed, except another cat, was another dog.

"How did that get in?" I asked Denny.

"Some children brought it to the door. They thought it might be ours."

I knew they hadn't thought any such thing. There wasn't a child in our block who didn't know everything that could be learned about us from outdoors—even about our bird nests and the dead gophers the cats left on the welcome mat. I wouldn't have been surprised to find that they looked at our mail.

"It's kind of cute, isn't it?" she said.

Obviously, the dog was a stray that the children's parents hadn't let them keep, but they knew my wife would take it in. Maybe they knew some things about her I didn't know. But she hadn't had good luck with dogs, and I wouldn't have thought she'd want to try again.

It was a female. I had to admit it was appealing. It was no more than three or four months old. About the size of a cocker, with a black and biscuit-colored coat of long silky texture.

"Do you know what it is?" Denny asked.

I ran through my computer. "Well," I said, "according to this it's either a Lhasa apso, a saluki, or a very small Afghan hound."

I decided it must be a Yorkshire terrier.

She called it Fluff.

22

My friend Herb Henrikson, an atomic physics engineer at the California Institute of Technology, designs the sort of machines in which experimental physicists catch elusive nuclear particles; for relaxation, he has a couple of Great Danes.

Having that kind of mind, Henrikson kept a detailed record of the expenses this hobby incurred, and after I bought my Airedale he showed me an itemized account of what the Danes had cost him in their first year of life.

One reason so many homemakers can't stay within their budgets is that they don't understand upkeep. There is an old folk-saying that all of us have heard: "It isn't the original cost, it's the upkeep." But upkeep is hard to figure in advance, and hard to account for afterward, unless you keep a book, the way Henrikson did. The invisible cost of upkeep, I imagine, is the phenomenon behind the common question, "Where did it go?"

The inability of the average American couple

to understand upkeep is what leads them to acquire automobiles, houses and dogs beyond their means.

I paid only $75 for my Airedale new, and had thought of him as a fairly inexpensive dog, considering his pedigree, until I received Henrikson's accounting on his Danes. Then I began to wonder if I hadn't overlooked a few things. Of course there were the expected fees for alterations and preventives, and he was eating like a lion. Once or twice I had him groomed at one of those dog beauty shoppes. He came out of it very handsome indeed, but the bill was $25, and that was before inflation. Finally I began to have him merely sheared, like a sheep, for less than a third the cost. He wouldn't win any ribbons, but I knew he wouldn't care, and if he didn't, I wouldn't either.

He was healthy enough, but now and then, like any animal in the city, he would get into trouble. One day he turned up with a limp, and I had to run him down to the dog and cat hospital, where Dr. Morehouse excised four foxtails from his right front paw. He had picked them up in Baja. It could have been worse. The bill was less than my dermatologist was charging to remove a tiny nodule from my forehead with an application of acid. Of course the dermatologist was dealing with a man's vanity, the veterinarian merely with a dog's pain and well-being.

All told, though, not counting food, I imagined he hadn't cost me much more than it would have cost to keep a Yamaha, for example, or a set of tennis rackets, if one played tournaments and had to have them restrung now and then.

But the Henrikson report set me to wondering. With the immaculate discipline expected of a laboratory scientist, he had kept a detailed account of what the Danes had cost from their purchase, at ten weeks, to their first birthday, as follows:

Purchase, $150; training, $115; doghouse, $210; foam rubber, $5; canvas,$10; denim, $8; bowls, leashes, balls, lunge line, choke chains, $22; spaying, $120; stomach surgery to remove six feet of clothesline Christmas morning, $150; jump through window (glass), $4, (stitches), $25; to halt undermining of the house (retaining wall), $675; (paving), $270; screen and bar windows, $30; single bed and mattress, $40; licenses, $15; food, $262; vitamins, $35; shots and treatment for virus, $50; structural aluminum reinforcement on front gate, $11.25; hose bib for watering dogs, $15; spot remover, $3.95; value of the oleander bushes they chewed to the nub, zero (they will grow back); protective fences for shrubs and young trees, $16; reupholstery of living room chairs (material only), $35.

The total (I took his word for it, since he had access to a computer out there at Caltech) was $2,277.70.

Thinking it over now, I see that the difference was not so much the difference between an Airedale and a Great Dane, as the difference between me and a scientist. If I had kept a detailed account of the Airedale's first year, including the times he ate the arms of the vinyl couch and chewed through the television cable under the house, he might have piled up as impressive a record as Henrikson's Danes. But by that time he was mature; his fires were banked, and I expected nothing worse of him from then on than the cost of his occasional and chaste misadventures.

I knew I might be in trouble, though, with the little stray my wife had taken in. Maybe I should keep a book on her. She weighed only ten pounds, but she seemed to think she was a Yorkshire terrier, and she had more vanity than a pair of Afghans.

One thing I didn't have to be a scientist to know: any female named Fluff was going to be expensive.

Though they never met, my Airedale and Henrikson's Danes were contemporaries, and they were alike in bringing comic relief into our lives, which helped to make them worth their keep.

Though Henrikson's scientific papers were over my head, now and then he wrote letters to me about his dogs in a style so unaffected but graphic that I wished these missives could have a greater audience.

I am gratified when I see a man of extraordinary intellect or virtue brought down to my own level of ineptitude and frustration by some everyday experience with animals, so here is one of Henrikson's reports, in his nonscientific words. It might be called "A Day at the Beach with Two Great Danes."

"Apropos your barking Airedale, stick, and being locked out, I had to drive my wife to the square in Venice, where she attended a watercolor seminar. For three hours I had to amuse our two Great Dane puppies (now eighty pounds each) during intermittent showers.

"They operate a continuous obedience class for me. They pull sharply on the leashes when they want me to run and they stop abruptly in my path when they want me to heel. They were chasing sea gulls along the water's edge. The gulls soared seaward with the dogs in mad pursuit. I could no more restrain them than the tin can tied to the rear of a newlywed couple's car could prevent their headlong dash toward that deep water.

"The dogs stopped short. I sailed over them, landing on my back in a foot of freezing, foaming, sandy brine, splashing madly for the loops on their leashes. At this point, on one of nature's occasional overkills, it began to rain.

"I sloshed up the beach toward the parking lot. With a newfound strength I dragged the two chariot horses to the car. Somewhere in my wet confusion I was planning on stuffing the dogs in the car, taking out a pair of dry pants from the trunk, changing in the car, and somehow regaining my status as a dues-paying member of the human race. I flung open the car door and began pushing the confused dogs in. It was like pushing two ribbons of toothpaste into a tube. At one point, I got a maximum of 1.5 dogs in. So much for the power of wet, blind fury.

"After a few calming, hyperventilating deep

breaths I got in the car myself. I called gently to them. I pulled on their leashes. No luck. At least this was an improvement. I was inside and they were standing out in the rain.

"In moments of stress sometimes a cliché comes to the rescue. I turned on KFAC and soon all three breasts were soothed. They stepped into the car and I leaped out and slammed the door. My dizzying sense of triumph was short-lived. With a deliberate squash of her massive paw one of the dogs depressed the lock button on the door. My keys were in the ignition. The dry pants would remain in the trunk. We stood there staring at each other. She turned calmly and planted both cabbage-like paws on the horn ring. Her sister licked a peephole in the fogged-up window and stared at me from the rear seat.

"In the introduction to his delightful book, *Man Meets Dog,* Konrad Lorenz speculates about the origin of the bond between man and dog. He describes the first time primitive man threw a piece of carrion to a starving pack of jackals to entice them to camp at the mouth of the cave and become the first sentry dogs.

"There followed the Stone Age, the Bronze Age, the Iron Age, the Written Word, the age of Athenean Greatness, Pax Romana, Camelot, the Renaissance, the Industrial Revolution and the century of the common man—hundreds of thousands of years of progress so that two dumb brutes could dump me in the Pacific, lock me out of my automobile in a rainstorm, scare the daylights out of me with their horn and then sit back and relax as Herbert von Karajan conducted Haydn's *The Seasons.*

"I suddenly remembered that I had a set of keys wired to a cable clamp in the engine compartment. I retrieved them but decided to cede the dogs the car, while I opted for a quiet drink in the Sandbar.

"I told my story to a lovely young lady whom I had never seen before. She responded sympathetically and asked me would I like to go home with her and have her prepare a nice hot meal. . . . My lower-middle-class morality and the fact that my wife would be looking for me in an hour helped make me realize that this was not a propitious day to break new ground. . . ."

As I say, it's gratifying to find out that even a physicist, whose mind takes flights that mine could never follow, is human enough to get locked out of his car by a dog and to surrender meekly to the harness of lower-middle-class morality.

23

I was surprised one Sunday morning when Sara Dalton phoned to ask me what to do about a peacock.

"You have one?" I asked.

"No," she said. "It's Allen, across the street."

She said the peacock had landed in his yard and wouldn't go away, and Allen didn't know what to do. Then he remembered that Sara was a friend of mine, and thinking that I was an expert, he asked her to ask me what to do about his peacock.

Oddly, I suppose I was rather an expert on peacocks. A few years earlier I had uncovered a story about a number of them that had escaped the Arboretum out in Arcadia, and walked along the Foothill Freeway (which was then under construction) to West Covina, a commuter suburb about fifteen miles to the east. Evidently they didn't like West Covina, though, and they went back to the Arboretum.

Also, as Dalton himself surely remembered, he and I had sighted a peacock one New Year's Day when we were sitting in my living room, waiting for the start of the Rose Bowl game on television.

Actually, it was Denny who saw it first. She had been outside tending her plants, trying to get them off to a good new year, I imagine. She ran into the house in a state closer to panic than I had ever seen her, and it should be noted that we were in Honolulu together the morning they bombed Pearl Harbor. She is not that easily upset.

As I remember that New Year's morning, though, she was almost inarticulate. She kept pointing to the sky, or the ceiling, since she was then inside the house, and shouting, "Caw. . . . caw! . . ."

Dalton and I, having been tranquilized by Bloody Marys, went out on the front porch and saw the cause of her unaccustomed loss of control. It was an extremely large bird. It had flown across our house and landed on the roof of the Gribble place across the street. It was so large that even in roosting it was awesome, and I could imagine that, in flight, it would be likely to upset even as steady a woman as my wife, not to mention Mrs. Dalton.

"Jesus and Mary!" said Dalton, who is not given to blasphemy, "it's a pterodactyl!"

That had been my first guess too. But then I remembered the peacocks that had escaped the Arboretum, and I realized that it was probably one of those. I won't say I wasn't disappointed. A pterodactyl-sighting would have done a lot more for my birdlist, not to mention my obituary, than a grackle.

"The thing to do," I told Mrs. Dalton when she called about the Allen peacock, "is to feed it."

"Feed it what?" she said.

"Insects."

"What kind?"

"Whatever kind are available."

"I'll tell him," she said.

"Tell him not to drive it off," I told her. "Just be nice to it."

After all, I thought, what was wrong with having a peacock? I wouldn't have minded having one myself; it could roost in the playhouse. Our grandchildren were fond of the playhouse, but they didn't come over very often, and in the interim the peacock could sit in it for them.

I made myself a Bloody Mary and watched the skies from our terrace, hoping the peacock would come over. Then I had a troublesome thought. I phoned Mrs. Dalton.

"I forgot to ask," I said. "Is it a male or a female?"

"Does it make any difference," she said, "other than the difference I'm thinking of?"

"It makes a difference in the way they look," I pointed out.

"Does that make any difference in what you do with them?" she asked.

"It's not what you do with it," I said. "It's what you call it. If it's a female, it should be called a peahen. Technically."

"Peacock is a generic term," said Mrs. Dalton. "It may be used in reference to a male or a female."

Of all our neighbors, Mrs. Dalton was one of the few who would have known that. It wasn't that she knew anything about peacocks at all, but she knew about the gender of nouns.

"It doesn't have any showy feathers," she said, "if that's what you mean."

It sounded as if she had turned feminist on me.

Mrs. Dalton phoned a day or two later to tell me the peacock was still around, and to warn me that I might get some flak for agreeing with her that the word peacock may stand for either sex. Though technically a peacock is a male, a peahen is a female, and the general term is peafowl.

Now a peacock is not a very rare bird over in Arcadia at the Arboretum. The resident flock, when the birds stay home, is so prolific that they have to be thinned out at public auction from time to time. But a peacock is rarely seen in most areas of Los Angeles, and the sight of one flapping its way over a residential neighborhood, from rooftop to rooftop, is disconcerting. They cast a frightening shadow, and the male is capable of the most bloodcurdling scream in nature.

Mrs. Dalton, despite her several virtues, is not a woman who keeps her poise when confronted by nature in the raw. I remember that she turned almost catatonic one Sunday when a gopher snake turned up in the yard outside her kitchen. Evidently, though, she had passed along my advice about feeding the peacock, because a neighbor named Erika soon turned up at the Thompson place, where the bird had settled in, with a pan of split peas.

There had been quite a commotion after that, and the next day I managed to get hold of Allen Thompson on the phone to find out what had happened. First, with several neighbor women showing up to give advice, the peacock had begun to behave erratically. It flew all about the Thompson house, which is a three-story wooden structure that offers many perches, and seemed to settle on a balcony with a view of Elysian Park.

Evidently tiring of this panorama, it flew down to the road and sauntered over toward the Dalton house. This is a rustic street, unpaved, and there isn't much traffic. Mrs. Dalton had naturally locked all her doors; the peacock looked all around, but couldn't get in.

Thinking he had got rid of the bird at last, Thompson drove down the hill to get his laundry, and when he came back he left his gate and front door open to bring some things into the house. It was sometime later, after he had shut the door and imagined himself secure, that Thompson started into his bathroom and found the peacock in occupancy. Evidently it had had to go to the bathroom, and had done so.

On Thompson's intrusion, however, it became excited, feeling itself cornered, I suppose, and tried to fly out the window. Since the window was screened, it was unable to make an exit, despite heroic efforts, and in a moment the room was full of feathers and objects knocked from Thompson's shelf of toilet articles. Thompson withdrew.

He might have been excused, at this point, for telephoning the proper agency for assistance, but in an emergency, of course, nobody can ever find the number of the proper agency. Besides, Thompson didn't want to report the bird; he merely wanted it off his hands.

The crisis was resolved by an off-duty policeman, as crises so often are, such fellows being men of action and accustomed to taking charge. In this case it was a man named Jim who lived nearby and kept animals and birds of exotic character as a hobby. This chap showed up carrying, with admirable foresight, a pillow slip.

"He knew how to get control of the wings," Thompson said, "which I didn't, and in a minute he had the bird in the pillow slip and took it away. His last comment was, 'I'll give it a good home.'"

That seemed to be the end of the affair, except for whatever static Mrs. Dalton and I might get over the use of the word peacock for a peahen. She said she had already been reprimanded by several of her friends, who insisted we were quite wrong, and she wanted me to be ready.

"Don't worry," I told Mrs. Dalton when she phoned. "It's pure pedantry to deny it. Anyway, you can tell them that this peafowl was a peacock."

We might have pursued the subject further, but suddenly Mrs. Dalton interrupted: "My God!" she shouted. "There's a cat going by the door with a gopher in its mouth!"

I wondered why the Daltons were talking about moving to the South Seas in the spring when Dalton retired, and leaving all the excitement they had right here on Mt. Washington.

A friend of mine named Work phoned me one day to ask a question about the sex of parakeets.

"What is it you want to know?" I asked.

"How do you tell a male parakeet from a female?"

"Why do you want to know?"

"I thought I might get a couple."

"Why?" I couldn't see Work with parakeets.

"Well, it's something to do. But I'm sort of embarrassed that I don't know how to tell one sex from the other."

"Don't let it bother you," I said. I told him about my problem with Fluff, the stray Yorkie my wife took in.

I wasn't sure whether it was a male or a female, and when I took it down to the vet's I didn't want to admit that to Tinker Belle. I simply put the dog down on the counter and said, "I'd like to have this dog fixed."

"You want him castrated?" she asked.

"If that's what you do."

She took the dog in her arms and gave it a quick onceover. "You want her spayed," she said.

I told Work I would be happy to phone my pet shop and ask them how you could tell a male parakeet from a female.

"I'd appreciate it," he said.

I looked up Hal's Pet Shop in my card file and

dialed the number, or thought I did. A woman answered.

"How do you tell a male parakeet from a female?" I asked.

There was a moment's silence. "This is the Anderson residence," she said at last.

I begged her pardon and looked the number up again and dialed it, being careful to get it right. A different woman answered. "Hal's pet shop."

"This is Jack Smith," I said.

"Mm hmm," she said, noncommittally.

"How do you tell the difference in sex between parakeets?" I asked.

"Well, to begin with," she said, "I'm an answering service. OK?" We both had a nervous laugh. "Hal's pet shop is closed," she added. "They'll be open tomorrow morning.

"But it isn't all that embarrassing," she went on, dropping the businesslike tone. "I had to find out myself. It's the color of that little hump over the beak. The only problem is, I don't remember which is which. I think if it's blue it's a male and if it's white it's a female. But I suggest very strongly that you check with Hal tomorrow morning."

I thanked her. "I'm supposed to be an expert myself," I said, "but I can't tell a parakeet from a sparrow."

"I won't tell anyone," she said. "Your secret is perfectly safe with me."

I phoned Work back and told him what I'd found out. We agreed that the information wasn't worth much until we found out which color meant which.

"I'll call Ralph Schreiber," I said. "He's curator of ornithology at the Natural History Museum. He ought to know."

Fortunately Schreiber was in. I asked him the question. "Let me call you back," he said. He called back. "All right, here it is. What we call a parakeet is not, in common usage, a parakeet. It's a budgerigar. The scientific name is really pretty—it's *Melopsittacus undulatus.*"

In breeding season, he went on, the fleshy spot at the base of the beak, called the cere, is dark blue in the male, brown in the female. But because there are numerous species, and much random breeding for color, this test is not reliable. He said there were two other ways by which even an unskilled observer could readily tell the difference. He told me what they were.

I called Work. I told him about the cere in breeding season, and described the other ways. "You have to watch them making love," I said, "and see which one's on top. In parakeets, that's the male. Or you watch and see which one lays an egg. Dr. Schreiber says if it lays an egg you're pretty sure it's a female."

"Well, thanks," he said. He didn't sound confident.

I saw his problem. Let's say he bought two parakeets and both of them were males. He could watch and watch, couldn't he, and never really know.

I sympathized with him. I had gone through it with goldfish.

24

We were having guests to dinner one Saturday night and I was hoping the wine glasses would arrive in time. A notice had come in the mail that we might expect them any day.

They were a set of six, glasses of the usual tulip shape, but unusual in their size. Each was large enough, as they had demonstrated to us at the winery, to hold a whole fifth-gallon bottle of wine.

I had won the set at a wine tasting a month or two earlier at the Italian Swiss Colony winery in Napa Valley. I had already forgotten what the contest was, but I had made some kind of good guess, and the prize was the set of glasses. They were to be sent express to our home.

They arrived on Friday, the day before the dinner party. I was late coming home Friday and it was Denny who found the wine glasses when she came home from work. It was an exciting moment for her, as I was to learn.

When I came home later I noticed at once that there was something odd about her. She looked as if she'd been in a scrap. She had a Band-aid on one hand and an eye that was bruised and going black.

"Did the wine glasses come?" I said. I never ask a person how she got a black eye.

She said yes, the wine glasses had come, and that was why she had a cut on her hand and a black eye.

"Where are they?" I asked. I knew she would explain when she was ready.

"There, on the bar."

They were enormous, shining in the dim light of the backbar, with the name and emblem of the winery etched on each.

"Don't you think they're ugly?" she asked.

"I think they're beautiful," I said. "Of course, it's in the eye of the beholder."

Suddenly it occurred to me that there were only five glasses, instead of the promised six. "What happened to the other one?" I asked.

That was the story. She had gone out into the dog yard to feed the dogs, knowing I wouldn't be home to do it, and had stepped on something crunchy and stooped to see what it was and the Airedale flew out of the dark and bumped her in the eye, knocking her down. Throwing out a hand to break her fall, she hit a shard of glass and got the cut.

Then she saw a large wine glass lying on its side, gleaming in the yard light, apparently unbroken. The Airedale was jumping all around it, expecting that he was about to get his dinner. He was joined by the poodles, leaping and yipping in their usual mindless frenzy.

She realized that the glass must be one of the expected wine glasses, and it was up to her to save it. She scooped up the unbroken glass before it joined the rubble underfoot, and retreated into the house, bleeding and seeing out of only one eye. She gave herself first aid, fed the dogs, and went out to search the yard.

She found what was left of the cardboard carton near the gate. It had been chewed open. Two of the compartments inside were empty. The Airedale had evidently managed to get the package open and extract two of the glasses, breaking only one. The others were inside, intact.

It was a mystery. What were the glasses doing in the dog yard in the first place?

It is my theory that the deliveryman, getting no answer at the front door, went around to the back of the house to leave the glasses, thinking they would be safer there. He must have thought it would be a brilliant idea to put them inside the dog yard fence, as thieves would be unlikely to risk an engagement with the Airedale. It was a good plan in theory, but a fiasco in practice.

I got a bottle of wine and opened it and poured it out into one of the new glasses. The glass held every drop. I poured half of it into a second glass and handed it to Denny.

"We might as well drink a toast," I said, "to our five new glasses."

"And one black eye," she said.

It could have been worse. She could have

stepped on the unbroken glass and we'd have had only four.

Seeing Denny the next few days with a black eye made me feel a bit guilty. Perhaps I was partly at fault in keeping Pugsley out of obedience school because I wasn't eager to see his exuberance curbed.

Even strangers had written to me urging that I give the Airedale some kind of training, insisting that it would make him a better dog without breaking his spirit.

One such letter came from a source whose integrity I did not question.

> Dear Mr. Smith,
> I belong to a club that deals exclusively with Airedales. . . . We are an Airedale Obedience Club only. It has been said that you are somewhat disenchanted with methods in obedience training. We would like an opportunity to change your mind in this area. I'm sure you will agree, to see a really happy and good working Airedale is a joy.
>
> We have been asked to do an obedience demonstration for an all-Airedale breed-handling class. If you ever have time, we would so enjoy having you attend one of our meetings either as a speaker or as an innocent bystander.
>
> Please come visit us.
> Laura S. Summers, Secretary
> Airedale Obedience Club
> of Southern California

After much soul searching, I answered as follows:

Dear Ms. Summers:
Thank you for the kind invitation to attend
one of your Airedale obedience classes.

If I did bring my Airedale, however, I'm
afraid you would have two innocent by-
standers, instead of one. I am obliged to say
that my Airedale, Fleetwood Pugsley, has
had so little obedience training that if he
were to see a group of fellow Airedales
demonstrating obedience he would be mystified, not to say demoralized.

Of course it isn't his fault, but mine. He
is an intelligent dog, and I'm sure he is eager to work, but there isn't much for him
to do around our place, and I haven't taught
him anything constructive.

The few things I have taught him are
negative. Don't do this. Don't do that. I have
taught him not to bark, for example, unless he sees something that he considers
worth calling to my attention. Thus, despite having as good a voice as any in the
neighborhood, he does not bark except at
wild animals, cats, other dogs, people and
the stars.

I have also taught him to sit on command. I know this is rather an elementary
skill, but it is not to be sneezed at when you
think of the alternatives. He is not a house
dog. I am unable to turn him out to run in
field and meadow, which is of course his

birthright as an Airedale, so the least I can do, it seems to me, is to keep him out of the house.

Consequently he has come to think of his fenced yard as indoors, and when the door is opened and he is let into the house, he naturally thinks he is being let outdoors, and he begins at once to go hunting for foxes or grouse or whatever it was his forebears hunted over there in England. In one minute he can disarrange the entire house, scattering rugs and overturning furniture until he has checked out every room. He naturally likes to bark while engaged in this sport, and so I am obliged to shout "Quiet!" and "Sit" until he finally skids to a stop in the kitchen.

It would indeed be wonderful to teach him to heel, so we could go on walks without a leash, but I just don't think I'm up to it. I'm tired by the time I get him to sit down and quit barking, and I don't think our lifestyle would accommodate obedience sessions.

Several friends have suggested that what we need rather than obedience training is psychiatric help, and I may get some, if I ever find a good man who likes us both.

Meanwhile, if you know of any obedience classes for women and poodles, please let me know.

Yours truly,
Jack Smith

Always alert for ways of improving Pugsley's life, within my limits and his, I discovered a world of services for dogs and cats that I had hardly known existed.

For example, I had supposed that the ultimate symbol of the adoration of dogs and cats in America was the pet cemetery, which Evelyn Waugh had satirized so devilishly in *The Loved One,* but I found out, from an ad in the paper, that there was also a pet church.

The ad appeared under the PETS classification, and read as follows:

"BAPTIZE YOUR PET!

"Solemnify the relationship between you and your pet by baptizing him. Have faith that your pet has a soul. Send $5 to have your pet's name permanently enrolled in the Universal religious community of pets. You will receive an engraved certificate of commemoration. Send your pet's name and breed, along with your name and address, to First Universal Pet Congregation, P. O. Box 3522, Merchandise Mart, Chicago, Ill. 60654."

Though I am not a profoundly religious person, I wouldn't want to reject out of hand any ritual that might bring a man and his dog spiritually closer together. My soul and the soul of my Airedale, if either of us had one, seemed to have parted company after I started training him not to bark.

But what worried me was the actual baptism. The ad in the paper didn't make it clear just what type of baptism was meant, and who was to perform the ceremony. I was inclined to doubt that for a mere five dollars any minister of the First

Universal Pet Congregation would undertake to baptize an Airedale, and certainly not if the FUPC required full submergence.

It was in fact my terror of full submergence that brought about my own escape from an early conversion to the Baptist Church of Bakersfield, California. My mother was intent on having me baptized at a tender age, before my father's heresies could reach me. However, she made the mistake of taking me to the church to see a dry run, or a wet run, I should say. I was so frightened by the spectacle of a lady in a white chiffon gown being lowered full-length into a tub of water that I declined to surrender when my turn came, enforcing my position with the threat of what was generally regarded as the most intimidating tantrum on our block.

As for solemnifying our relationship, I doubted that we could do that simply by having Pugsley baptized. I imagined that I would have to be baptized too, and I was even less inclined then to let some clergyman lower me into a tub than I had been at the age of five.

Also, the First Universal Pet Congregation asked us to send our pet's name and breed. Of course Fleetwood Pugsley was a purebred dog, and had his papers. But I felt that if the FUPC didn't accept mongrels, then it wasn't the faith for us. If Fleetwood Pugsley did indeed have a soul, it was perhaps revealed in his absolutely democratic acceptance of other dogs, pedigreed or not. Neither of us had the slightest interest in joining an exclusive church.

Furthermore, if Pugsley and I had wanted to join a dog church we certainly wouldn't have joined one with an address such as "Merchandise Mart, Chicago." Merchandise Mart had a commercial ring I didn't like, and Chicago seemed to me the least likely city in America for the rooting of a new religion. It was too cold and windy, for one thing, and sultry in the summer.

I had an idea that if God had wanted to start a church for dogs he would have started it in Los Angeles.

So Fleetwood Pugsley, like his master, was never baptized.

25

Though I have tried to make it clear that I am not a bird expert, people continue to write me questions about birds. One unusual query concerned not only birds but also butterflies, which I know even less about than birds.

> Dear Mr. Smith:
> My parents, Charlotte and Frank Haskell, very sensible people in their 80s, have been telling me that butterflies chase birds—that the birds fly off in terror. This seems to happen mostly with a large black butterfly. We agreed that I would write and ask you if you had ever heard of this. Many thanks.
> Barbara MacEvoy

My first impulse was to suggest that Mrs. MacEvoy write the museum. But it occurred to me that even a novice could tell whether butterflies chased birds or not, simply by watching. Besides, I'd been down for two days with a bad throat. Watching butter-flies would be a good way to get back into action. I got up early the next morning and sat in my swivel chair in front of our picture window and Denny brought me some toast, orange juice and coffee and I began work.

The first butterfly I saw was orange with black spots. A Gulf fritillary, I guessed. I tried to keep my eye on it, which wasn't easy. Now and then it stopped to rest, but there was no point in watching when it was resting, as it wouldn't be resting and chasing birds at the same time.

While I had my eye on the Gulf fritillary, a white butterfly fluttered by. How interesting, I thought—that phrase. A butterfly fluttered by? That must be the etymology of the word! It had once been flutterby, and somehow it had gotten turned around into butterfly.

I went into the den and looked up butterfly in Webster's. It said the word came from the Old English buterfloege (butter plus fly), "perhaps from the belief that butterflies or witches in the shape of butterflies stole milk and butter."

A preposterous conjecture if I'd ever heard one. I turned to the *Oxford English Dictionary*. "The reason for the name," said OED, "is unknown." That was more like it. The English lexicographers evidently hadn't thought of "flutter by," as I had; but at least they hadn't fallen for the butter-eating witch theory, an obvious canard.

When I returned to my post the white butter-fly was gone. Two hawks were circling over the canyon. Dalton's red-tails, probably. I was about to put the glasses on them when a black butterfly fluttered by. My heart thumped. This was it.

Just then the jay came back. The black butterfly left its perch. By George, I thought, it's going to chase the jay! The butterfly made a feint toward the jay, but evidently changed its mind and lurched off in another direction.

That was good enough for me. It had had its chance, unless it was crazy enough to go for the hawks. I had my answer.

Dear Mrs. MacEvoy:
Though I am more of an etymologist than an entomologist, I have gone to some pains to answer your question. You may put your parents' minds to rest. Butterflies do not chase birds. They do not, in any case, chase scrub jays. To go beyond this tentative conclusion I would have to do more field work.

However, it may interest you and your parents to know that, in the course of the study prompted by your question, I enjoyed a serendipitous and most gratifying etymological insight. The word butterfly is derived from the phrase flutter by, used in early times, I should imagine, to describe this charming insect's mode of locomotion.
Your servant,
Jack Smith

By luck, the International Lepidopterists Society was in town for its annual meeting when I published my open letter to Mrs. MacEvoy. Naturally my opinion caused some excitement and a little controversy among the visiting butterfly and moth people, and as a result I was invited to attend their banquet at the Natural History Museum.

I was delighted. It was an honor being asked to break bread with perhaps the most distinguished lepidopterists in the world; the more so as lepidoptery was a field in which I had not previously published. Also, I hoped I might glean more evidence to support my conclusion that butterflies don't chase birds.

When I arrived there were perhaps a hundred persons gathered in the foyer around the rampant dinosaur skeletons. I got a drink and moved among them. Julian Donahue, the museum's moth man, introduced me to a distinguished-looking white-haired gentleman named Arthur Allyn, an amateur from Sarasota, Florida.

"Mr. Allyn can tell you something about butterflies chasing birds," said Donahue.

"I saw it happen," Allyn said. "We have a bird show in our jungle garden, outside the museum. Trained cockatoos. Very smart birds. Well, this yellow cockatoo was riding a scooter, and all of a sudden this *Papilio cresphontes* flew down in front of him, flapping its wings."

"Papilio what?" I asked.

"Cresphontes. That's a big swallowtail, brown and yellow. Size of your hand."

"What happened?"

"Well, it just scared hell out of the cockatoo. He screamed bloody murder and fell off his scooter."

It was bad news. My first paper was compromised. However, I told myself, one incident doesn't prove or disprove a hypothesis.

A few days later I received this letter from Busch Gardens, a popular, jungle-like amusement park that Anheuser-Busch used to run for the public next door to its brewery in the west San Fernando Valley—before it found something more profitable to do with the land. The park had streams and fountains, and unlike Disneyland's, its tropical birds were real, though their wings were clipped.

> Dear Mr. Smith:
> I was interested in your comments about butterflies chasing birds. I perform in the bird show at Busch Gardens with trained cockatoos and macaws. One week recently we seemed to have attracted a butterfly, and during the bird show he teased the cockatoos, getting close enough to frighten them but not close enough to be eaten. One of the birds counts on a bell; he was distracted constantly, and at times he ran from the harmless butterfly.
> I thought I would tell you this to confirm Mr. Allyn's statement about his cockatoo being frightened. . . .
> Yours truly,
> Barbara Firestone

Before I accepted Allyn's story about the cowardly Florida cockatoo, I'd need some verification from my own experience. Miss Firestone had opened the door to just that.

I drove out to Busch Gardens in time for the one o'clock bird show. A young woman came out and said she was Barbara and introduced the birds. The show began. A blue and gold macaw named Laura led off with a prayer, then flew upside down. A macaw named Michael rolled over, a trick that didn't impress me much, as almost any dog can be taught to do it.

It was when Miss Firestone brought the cockatoos out that I tensed up. They were all white with yellow crests, like Allyn's bird in Sarasota. They warmed up on a merry-go-round, and Clyde, the star, rode a scooter across the stage. He reached the far side without mishap.

Then Miss Firestone raised him to the high wire. He mounted a bicycle and started pedaling across the wire. He was hardly halfway over when my eye caught a dark fluttering above the amphitheater, at nine o'clock high. The adrenalin hit me. Was this it?

It was only a leaf. Clyde reached the other side of the wire. The crowd applauded, unaware of the drama they had missed.

The rest was routine. Edward did some addition and subtraction, giving his answers on a bell. Robin got herself locked up in a castle. Homer fired a cannon at the castle and set it on fire. Edna rushed up a ladder to put the fire out and rescue Robin, and Big Ed raised the American Flag. The show was over.

Naturally I was disappointed. I was hoping for a convincing demonstration.

Meanwhile, I received a letter from Professor John W. McMenamin of the department of biology at Occidental College, recalling a vivid boyhood memory of a butterfly attacking a bird.

"I was collecting insects on an abandoned studio lot in Hollywood when a sudden movement overhead attracted my attention. There against the clear blue sky a monarch butterfly was striking a blackbird in flight—two, three, four times—before the faster-flying bird was out of range. . . ."

Professor McMenamin said he had discussed this incident with a colleague, Dr. Patrick H. Wells, who was then engaged in a study of the monarch's life-style.

Wells told him:

"In breeding season a stimulated male will attempt to mate with any available female by pouncing on her in flight. If no female is available, the contact may be made with another moving object such as a falling leaf. . . ." Or a blackbird.

"With this information in mind," Professor McMenamin concluded, "I suggest the hypothesis that the reported interactions of butterflies and birds are isolated incidents of misplaced amorous behavior by male butterflies."

Oh, well, since when has a bird been safe in Hollywood?

I dropped my inquiry. That kind of field work was for a younger person.

26

A young woman whom I will call Mrs. Hirsch was a defendant recently in a criminal case similar to one in which my wife and I were enmeshed years ago, and I think some interesting insights into the judicial temperament may be had from a comparison of the two.

I heard of the Hirsch case through Dr. Eric Webb, a professor of anesthesiology at UCLA, an occupation which is irrelevant to the case except as it tends to establish Dr. Webb's probable reliability as a witness. He said the young woman is a talented artist and "a very beautiful redhead," which may have been a significant factor.

Briefly, Mrs. Hirsch was accused of permitting a dog on the beach at Santa Monica, a misdemeanor. The dog happened to be the Webb dog, a Dalmation named Shandy. The Webbs had gone out of town, and Mrs. Hirsch had agreed to care for Shandy in their absence.

It was a lovely day, according to the story I finally drew from Mrs. Hirsch herself over the telephone, and she decided to take the Dalmatian for a romp on the beach, not knowing it was against the law. She did have the dog on a leash, however.

"We were having such fun," she said. "There was nobody else in sight."

Then, unfortunately, the dog committed a faux pas, the possibility of which, of course, is the main reason dogs are not permitted on the beach in the first place.

"All of a sudden we heard a siren," said Mrs. Hirsch, "and this policeman rushed over."

In her opinion, the policeman overplayed his role, scolding her and the dog in a rude and truculent manner. "The dog was so embarrassed," Mrs. Hirsch said.

She told the officer that the dog was not her dog; that she had never owned a dog in her life; that the dog was a guest in her home, and looked to her for protection from rude policemen; that there were no signs posted; that the dog was on a leash, as the officer could plainly see, and that it was a lovely day.

Given these persuasive considerations, and adding the probability that Mrs. Hirsch was indeed a very beautiful redhead, one might have excused the officer for letting her off with a warning. But he wrote a ticket; technically, none can blame him.

Mrs. Hirsch went to court in Santa Monica. She had never been in court before. She waited two hours while the judge disposed of drunk driving cases and other heavy misdemeanors. Finally her case was called. Having no lawyer, she declined the services of the public defender and pleaded guilty, offering the same list of extenuating circumstances she had recited to the officer.

Moved by the merit of her argument, or by the sweet reason with which it was delivered, or only, perhaps, by her redhaired beauty, the judge suspended sentence, and Mrs. Hirsch went free.

"He was very nice," she said.

Now in the case of the *People vs. Jack Smith and Denise Smith,* we were cited for allowing our dog Shaggy to run about in the neighborhood off leash. It was Denny, though, who went to court (for the first time in her life) since her name was on the citation as well as mine, and I was quite busy.

She, too, waited hours, but it was at the Lincoln Heights Jail court, downtown, instead of Santa Monica. It was the kind of courtroom where the jetsam of society shows up; a dreary stream of prostitutes, drunks and pickpockets; life's losers; the beaten, the downtrodden and the dispossessed.

It was among this riffraff that my wife appeared one morning to answer to a charge of violating the dog leash law. You will know how long ago this was when I tell you that she wore white gloves and a hat: a very smartly turned out matron for her first appearance in the dock. In that motley backwash she stood out like an I. Magnin model in a breadline, and I was hoping that the judge would be impressed by such obvious class and be inclined to leniency. It isn't that a chic defendant is any more entitled to justice than a seedy one; but all of us males have an old-fashioned touch of gallantry, even judges.

It was two hours before she was called. She told her story. Her codefendant in the case was technically me, but in a larger sense it was Shaggy, whose indiscretions had gotten us into trouble once before.

My wife told the judge we were always careful to keep Shaggy at home, along with her ne'er-do-well son Blaze, but in the instance for which she now stood before him, they had both gotten out at the same time and run in opposite directions. At that time Denny was fleet of foot and, being more intelligent than the dogs, she was able to catch them, one at a time. This time, however, the dogcatcher just happened to be cruising the neighborhood and he captured Shag while my wife was running in the opposite direction after Blaze.

She had planned to tell the judge the dog was actually taken by the dogcatcher on our own sidewalk, which was true, and to produce a dozen schoolchildren to testify that they had witnessed this event on their way home from school. But when she saw the courtroom she knew it was not a fit place for children, and abandoned that defense.

I pointed out that it had not been prudent to bring Blaze into the story, since it revealed that she had been guilty of letting two dogs loose, not just the one, but of course it was the truth.

Certainly it showed that she had done her best, and I thought the story might move the judge to let her off with a warning. She did look quite attractive. But he'd had a long unpleasant morning, and perhaps his milk of human kindness had run dry.

He fined her $10, with the option, which was routine, of going to jail. I thought she ought to have gone to jail, just to make the judge feel guilty and perhaps move him to reconsider. But she didn't want to take that chance, and she paid. At the time, it hurt.

Years later, when I read in the paper one day that the California State attorney general intended to "purge" the State Department of Justice's files of personal records that were no longer "relevant," I was heartened. Her loose dog conviction—the only criminal mark on her escutcheon—could at last be expunged, in the name of justice.

"We are after those records of a person who might have gotten into trouble years ago," he said, "but has been law abiding ever since. Saving an ancient record of a youthful indiscretion serves no purpose in the criminal justice system."

That statement of intention suited Denny's case precisely. She had certainly been rehabilitated. After that degrading day in court she had never again relaxed her vigilance, and none of our dogs was ever picked up again.

It was an enlightened move on the attorney general's part. There are few of us, I imagine, who don't have at least one "youthful indiscretion" in our past, some little embarrassment, the record of which we would be happy to have destroyed. Even my own box score has not been free of errors.

Also, there was a wonderful justice in the attorney general's proposal of amnesty as it applied to my wife, for neither of us had ever forgotten the name of the judge who sat that day in that lowly court, dispensing justice to the dregs of the city, and behold, he was now attorney general of the State of California—himself!

From that mean post in the jailhouse courtroom, he had risen to become the top policeman in the state—the very apotheosis of the man of law and, in a sense, the state's top dogcatcher, too. His career had been impeccable, and I had no doubt that it was rooted in the kind of integrity that had obliged him to close his eyes to my wife's chic and her station, and mete out justice as her crime deserved.

I doubt that the judge who let Mrs. Hirsch off so easily in Santa Monica will go very far. He's too soft on redheads.

27

Every March, for several years, I would receive a letter from Henry Childs, the birdman of Chaffey College, urging me, before it was too late, to expose the legend of the swallows of San Juan Capistrano as a fraud.

As everyone knows (or believes, I should say) the swallows come back to the mission of San Juan Capistrano on March 19. This phenomenon has come to rank not far behind the Resurrection as an article of Christian faith; and it has also been very useful to San Juan Capistrano as a tourist attraction, though I cannot understand why anyone would go out of his way to see as plain a bird as the cliff swallow, even in large numbers.

One March, after receiving a particularly anguished appeal from Childs, I decided that he deserved a hearing. To give an idea of the depth of Childs' feeling about it, I quote from one of his letters:

"Attack this windmill—destroy the myth as only you can do and then on to bigger things! Do not fail in this hour of truth!"

He then went on about the swallow: "Like many other migrating songbirds, its northern migration is markedly affected by the weather. It should also be noted that the migratory urge has been shown to be a result of gonadal enlargements caused by the short ending of the day length. That the swallows return to Capistrano due to this sort of discomfort has not received the attention which our sexually oriented society usually gives to such phenomena.

"It is interesting to note that almost without fail, some swallows do return to Capistrano on March 19. Why is this? Could it be that the newspaper reporters, the TV newscasters, and thousands of gullible citizens are there to observe their arrival, and at no other time? As one who has been at Capistrano on March 9, and by actual count seen more than 500 swallows, and then read in the paper about their prompt arrival on March 19, I am not a believer in this myth. . . ."

I certainly respected Childs' opinions, but in the interest of journalistic if not scientific inquiry, I decided to check it out myself.

As Childs had done, I drove down to Capistrano a few days in advance of March 19 to see if any swallows had arrived prematurely at the mission.

"How are you going to count them?" my wife asked as I was finishing my coffee.

"I'll just count them—one, two, three," I said.

"I mean, do you know what a swallow looks like?"

She had a point. I found my copy of *Peterson's Field Guide* and looked up the cliff swallow, which is the kind that comes to Capistrano. "Note the rusty or buffy rump," it said. "Overhead, the bird appears squaretailed with a dark throat patch. Glides in a long ellipse, ending each glide with a much steeper climb than other swallows. Voice: a low chur."

Denny pointed to a tiny gold bird hanging at her throat from a gold chain. "This is what they look like," she said. It looked like the picture of the cliff swallow in Peterson's book, with a squared-off tail.

It was a fine day, like spring, and I wouldn't have been surprised to find hundreds of swallows already in residence at the mission. Their scouts might easily have been fooled by that year's February warm spell.

I parked in front of the mission and paid a dollar to go in. Inside the walls the gardens and cloisters were cool and quiet, shaded by ancient trees. There were few visitors. The hordes would descend on Thursday, the 19th. The old stones and bricks of the ruins were sharply textured in the brilliant sunlight; the bougainvillea and geraniums were shocking pink; the goldfish hardly moved in the tepid fountain pool.

Almost at once I saw a number of birds on the crown of the ruined stone church. The roof and walls had crumbled after the earthquake of 1812, but the towering sanctuary was almost intact, and the birds were perched on its top, from which they launched themselves on short impulsive flights.

A pair of them came gliding down toward the fountain where I stood, and suddenly climbed. It was exquisite, breathtaking, and for a moment I thought I had seen my first swallows. I listened for a low chur. They were too swift for me to check their rumps.

I walked over toward the ruin. I am not very good at identifying birds, but I do know a pigeon when I see one close enough. The birds on the ruin were pigeons; some dark and pearl gray, some pure white. Not another kind of bird was in sight.

I went into the gift shop and bought a little blue swallow pin for 99¢, but it was the wrong species. It had a tail like a swallow-tail coat, which is something else.

"Have you seen any swallows yet?" I asked the woman at the counter.

"Haven't seen one," she said, looking me straight in the eye.

I bought a packet of pigeon food and sat on a bench. It is said that the Capistrano pigeons will eat out of your hand. I scattered some of the seed on the ground, thinking they might see it. They ignored me. Suddenly I knew I had company. A sparrow was working its way toward my feet, two steps forward, one back, quick, alert, calculating the risk against the prize. It began picking at the seed. That sparrow, I swear, was the only bird I saw in San Juan Capistrano on March 16, except the pigeons.

It didn't prove that Childs was wrong, of course. But if the swallows did show up in force on Thursday, I would have to be a believer.

On March 19 I got up early and drove down to Capistrano once more. When I pulled off the freeway I was disheartened to see a block-long line of people waiting to get into the mission. The streets were clogged with cars and tour buses.

I found a place to park two blocks away and walked back to the mission and accosted a middle-aged couple as they pushed through the exit turnstile.

"Did you see any swallows?" I asked.

"Not yet," the woman said. "They're coming later."

"There's too many people," the man said. "It scares them off."

I paid my dollar and went in. It was fiesta. Eight mariachis in silver-spangled black pants and embroidered cream jackets were playing to an audience of several hundred, ranging from wizened old women to infants in strollers. A young woman with a set of oil paints sat in a deck chair by the fountain, coloring and selling souvenir drawings of the mission. Ladies at tables were selling turquoise jewelry, clay pots, baskets, Indian dolls, coffee, hot dogs, soda pop and popcorn.

I studied the ruin of the old church on which the pigeons had been roosting three days earlier. They were still there, in command of the high ground. Not a swallow in sight.

"You have to look up high," I heard one old lady explaining to another. "They don't like people." They both looked hopefully upward.

In what would have been the nave of the crumbled church a television crew was setting up, two men, facing each other, one with a camera on his shoulder, the other with a mike in his hand. A stocky woman in a light blue polyester pantsuit with a swallow pin on one shoulder peered at the logo on the camera. "KGTV San Diego," she read aloud. "I'm from Massachusetts."

"Have you seen any swallows?" the cameraman asked her.

"Personally, I haven't looked," she said. "I've been too busy taking pictures."

"Me too," the cameraman said.

"I've seen an awful lot of pigeons," the woman said.

The reporter said he was ready for a test and began to talk into the mike. "There is a lot more to the fiesta of Las Golondrinas," he said in his on-screen voice, "than pageantry, tradition and the mission. . . . Yes, a lot more—it's called taking care of business. . . ."

I moved on. It seemed too festive a day for such a note of cynicism.

Back at the entrance, a group of fifty or sixty boys and girls had just arrived and were being made to sit in uneasy order on the ground. Suddenly one or two of them shouted "There they are!" and pointed skyward. A thrill seemed to run through the group.

I turned and looked up too, my own pulse quickening.

It was only pigeons.

When I got out on the sidewalk I checked my watch. Twelve minutes after noon. St. Joseph's Day was half over, and I hadn't seen a swallow yet. I had to get back to Los Angeles. I couldn't wait it out.

At a dinner that evening one woman told me she had heard on the radio that the swallows had come back, another told me she had heard that they hadn't.

The next morning I phoned the San Juan Capistrano Chamber of Commerce and talked to Doris Lindsey, the manager. "Did the swallows come back?" I asked.

"Oh, they certainly did. They always do."

I told her I hadn't seen any.

"Oh, they may not descend in flocks on the mission," she said. "They came in at 9:15 in small groups. With all the activity at the mission they probably were hiding. But they're all around town."

Anyway, it's a wonderful place to watch pigeons.

28

I wouldn't mention my lumbosacral trouble except that it seems to be the one thing I have in common with almost everyone else.

As Shakespeare wrote, "One touch of nature makes the whole world kin." (Scholars tell us that the "touch of nature" Shakespeare had in mind was jealousy, but how do they know he wasn't referring to Othello's lower back pain?)

I have had back pain since adolescence, but the problem suddenly became serious after an incident in which I was trying to help Jolie, the poodle. As a result of that humane but reckless impulse, my right leg has turned numb, the right foot quickly tires and begins to hurt when walking, and I have lost much of my natural grace and agility.

It strikes me as a good reflection on my generosity of spirit, if not my intelligence, that the two most painful back injuries I have suffered in recent years both occurred while I was engaged in acts of good will.

The first one came when I was lifting my wife's Mother's Day present out of the trunk of my car. It was a Cuisinart, in a large cardboard carton, and in leaning forward into the trunk and lifting and twisting the weight sideways, I put too great a strain on the lumbar region. It may have been this accident that weakened the muscles and left me more vulnerable to the second one.

The accident involving the poodle occurred during another spring rain. A strange situation had developed among our dogs. Usually, Pugsley still stood out in the rain, scorning shelter, while Jolie and Fluff took refuge in their houses. But this had been an unusually wet year. Often there was thunder and lightning, and Pugsley sometimes gave up his communion with the elements and sought shelter—not in the larger house which he shared with the Yorkie, but, perversely, in the smaller one with the poodle.

Since the loss of her brother, Jolie had gone her independent way. If the others tried to enter her house she snarled, which usually kept them out. Fluff, on the other hand, had attached herself to Pugsley. She was his companion and shadow, and they shared the larger house amiably.

Why, then, did Pugsley suddenly turn his back on this arrangement and commandeer Jolie's dog-house when it rained?

There was room enough in the house for both, though to get in and out its smaller door the Airedale had to squeeze up like a man being shot out of a cannon. However, for reasons of her own, the poodle chose not to stay in the house when the

Airedale came in. He was the gentlest of dogs, and would not deliberately have done anything to drive her out, but apparently she simply didn't care to live with him.

Thus I discovered that whenever the Airedale moved in, the Poodle nested under the hibiscus tree, which had always been a favorite retreat for all the dogs. One evening when I went out to feed them she emerged from that bosky haven, wet as a frog and obviously out of sorts.

I brought her inside and dried her with Denny's hair dryer and let her stay in the service porch in a cardboard carton. However, I don't think poodles should be pampered, so the next morning, the storm having let up, I put her out. That evening it was the same. I found her under the hibiscus, and Pugsley in her house. That is when I hurt myself.

I coaxed Pugsley out of the house. I squatted and lifted the poodle, placing the palm of my left hand under her belly, and then reached out with the other hand and picked up a twelve-inch cement block that unfortunately happened to be standing there unattached, thinking I would set it in the door of the doghouse sideways to keep the Airedale out, but leaving room enough for the poodle to get in. A harebrained scheme. As I moved, with these two weights in my outstretched hands, twisting to set the block in the doghouse doorway, there was a deep quivering pain in my lower back and I knew I had done something more serious than I had ever done before.

This time Dr. Reap sent me to an orthopedist. As the orthopedist studied my X rays I started to tell him the story. But he was a busy doctor, and I realized he didn't need to know about the Airedale having tired of the rain, and turning out to be anathema to the poodle, and my own ethical attitudes. All he wanted to know was what I had done, not why.

"I stooped over and lifted a wet dog with one hand," I said, "and a cement block with the other, and moved the block sideways across my body."

He nodded, as if I had described some sort of classic maneuver.

I also thought I ought to tell him about the time I fell out of the Moana Hotel at Waikiki Beach during World War II. He listened solemnly. That probably accounted, he conjectured, for the fact that one of my vertebral disks was shot, like a bad shock absorber.

"I'm going to put you in a corset for three weeks," he said.

He wrote out a prescription for a lumbosacral corset, if I remember the word, and sent me down the street to a place that sold such things.

I was fitted by a woman. "Take your shirt off," she said, "and let your pants down."

She put me into a straitjacket that had four steel snaps and three hooks down the front, steel braces in the back, and straps and buckles over the hips, to be drawn tight. She snapped me up and drew me tight. I got the impression that she was slightly amused. But I felt like a medieval bride being fitted into her chastity belt by a husband who was leaving on a Crusade.

The corset was a drag. I don't see how women ever wore them purely out of vanity and fashion. Also, I had arthritis that made it painful to put too much stress on my fingers. I couldn't close the snaps on the thing, so my wife had to lock me in it every morning. I got the impression that she too was slightly amused.

But there were compensations. I couldn't bend over while I had the corset on, so she had to pick up for me, and naturally she had to feed the dogs.

The next time it rained the problem was hers.

The corset didn't help. My symptoms grew worse, and finally X rays of my lower back after a dye had been injected into the spinal column revealed a massive rupture of the fourth vertebral disk. Surgery was essential and urgent.

The irony of my predicament, of course, was that the accommodation I had been trying to contrive for Jolie's comfort when I ruptured the disk probably wouldn't have worked anyway. It had been a foolish impulse, doomed to failure.

In my post-surgical idleness, I had plenty of time to ponder the cards and letters I was receiving, only a few of which, alas, were get-well messages. The others did little to relieve my pain, which for five weeks, night and day, was unrelenting.

"There is justice in the world," wrote someone who signed only the initials A.L. "That darling little poodle should have been inside—sleeping on the foot of your bed. Also the terrier. Yes, even the Airedale. You deserve a bad back. May you suffer for your sins."

"Why would you let the Yorkie and poodle out in the rain in the first place?" wrote a Mrs. K.S. "We have a miniature poodle that will be fourteen years old in May. We would not think of letting our dog get wet. . . ."

"I am dismayed," wrote the president of an animal assistance league, "that someone of your sensitivities would make his poodle and Yorkshire terrier sleep outside, particularly in the recent bad weather. . . . However, allowing that most dogs, like most people, can adapt to almost any environment, I still don't understand why the Airedale does not have his own doghouse. It is one of the first responsibilities of a pet owner to ensure that the pet has a place of his own, sheltered from the elements. If you have any difficulty obtaining a doghouse, our league might be able to provide one through its Pet-Aid Program."

I didn't wish to seem ungrateful for those expressions of concern, even though they weren't for me, but I did try to point out one or two misconceptions.

First, my Airedale had a doghouse. It was the Yorkie that didn't have a doghouse. But the Yorkie wouldn't have stayed in her own doghouse. She wanted to be in the Airedale's doghouse. And the Airedale had always seemed willing to share. After all—people share.

Also, once again I reminded them that both the

Airedale and the poodle were made of hardy stuff. To let either of them sleep at the foot of a bed would have been an insult to their heritage and their pride, and probably have undermined their health.

As for the Yorkie, just the word Yorkshire evokes pictures of this jaunty creature romping over the moors, happy as an eel in its frigid ponds, exulting in freedom from the castle walls.

No, I still think these breeds are happier outdoors. If I wanted an inside dog, first I'd build a fireplace. Then I'd get a couple of bull mastiffs, or maybe Great Danes, to lie beside it. Now those are my idea of house dogs.

29

Pugsley was no longer a young dog when at last we considered ourselves able to build a swimming pool. That's when we found out how expensive an Airedale can be.

I was reminded of Herb Henrikson's account of how much it was costing him to raise his two Great Danes. The way our bills for Pugsley mounted, simply in connection with the pool construction, I no longer felt as much sympathy for my friend.

First, the old chain-link fence had to be torn out. It stood astride the pool site, and we wanted to put in a larger fence to enclose a greater portion of our acre. This meant we had to make temporary arrangements for the dogs, especially Pugsley.

I thought of chaining him for the time being. If I turned him loose he would be two blocks away in thirty seconds. I knew Jolie and Fluff would stay close to home if the Airedale wasn't free to lead them astray.

It was a perfectly practical scheme, meant only as a stopgap. As soon as the pool was finished we would put up the new fence around the entire backyard, and he would have the run of it. I do not like to chain a dog, but it was necessary for Pugsley's own safety to keep him off the street and out from under cars. The price of having kept him in the yard all those years was that he had never developed any street smarts. But in the end I couldn't do it. I simply couldn't put a chain on an Airedale.

The alternative was to board all three dogs at our dog and cat hospital. Denny drove them down the hill and signed them in. I knew it would be expensive, just as a week in Good Samaritan Hospital would be more expensive than a week in the Biltmore Hotel. But I thought it would be a good chance for them all to get their shots and a checkup, and Tinker Belle could keep an eye on them.

It was a good plan. The dogs would have been frightened and unmanageable, I'm sure, when the bulldozer was in the yard scooping out the hole for the pool. Then we had the steel man and the plumber and the electrician and the Gunite crew and the numerous other specialists who have to be brought in for a swimming pool.

With all the activity, I forgot about the dogs until one day when I was discussing the fence with the fence man. We would not only have to build a five-foot fence around the entire backyard, but also an interior fence to keep the dogs out of the pool itself.

Suddenly I wondered how they were, and if the vet had begun to think we had abandoned them. I phoned to find out. "They're fine," Tinker Belle told me.

"By the way," I said, "how much are we paying? Five or six dollars a day?"

"It's ten dollars," she said.

I sent my wife down the hill to bring them home. The bill was $320. I'm not complaining. As I say, we were paying for medical attention as well as board and room. But $320 was more than I had meant to put into the pool in behalf of the dogs.

The cost of that portion of the fence which would be required simply to contain the Airedale was $1,067.13.

Unless providence intervened, there was nothing to do, for the time being, but to take him back to the hospital, or chain him after all.

As I had hoped, providence intervened. Our daughter-in-law Gail couldn't bear the thought of Pugsley being chained up, so she offered to take him for the duration.

I didn't want to sound too eager when she phoned, so I reminded her that although he was gentle, he was also large and exuberant, and might knock her down out of sheer good will. She was then expecting her second child, rather soon, and I didn't think she needed an Airedale to add to her perils.

Also, I pointed out, any strange dog, and especially one larger than themselves, might not be welcomed by her own dogs, Pepper and Sadie. Pepper was an Australian sheepdog and Sadie, as I have noted, was some kind of tiny mongrel, possibly a cross between a fox terrier and a Chihuahua. They were both rather flighty females, spoiled by attention and house privileges (in my opinion, which was not popular), and I was afraid they would resent the intrusion of an older male Airedale who hadn't had a bath or a haircut in months.

"I don't think there'll be any problem," she said. "If there is you can always take him back."

"She wants to take Pugsley," I told Denny, hardly able to hide my relief.

Denny drove Pugsley over to Gail's house on a Saturday morning and when she came home she had our granddaughter Alison.

"What's this?" I said, opening the door to find the little girl on our threshold, looking wide-eyed and energetic.

"Gail made us a deal," my wife said. "She takes Pugsley and we take Alison."

"You're kidding," I said, common sense quickly overcoming an irrational moment of alarm.

"It's only overnight," she said. "We're invited over for dinner tomorrow."

"Pom-pom," Alison said.

"What's she saying?" I asked.

"She's saying grandpa."

I couldn't believe it. "I didn't know she could speak English yet," I said.

I had work to do that evening and shut myself in my study, but my security consists only of two louver doors that can be opened by a determined push or an accidental impact, such as that made by a body bumping into them. When this is done they fly back and slam against the wall on either side with a sound like pistol shots.

I was staring at a sheet of paper in my typewriter, trying to get my thoughts in focus, when the doors flew open and slammed against the wall like pistol shots. My granddaughter lurched in, fell to her knees like a comic in the Ice Follies, pushed herself upright, and gave me a devastating smile. She is an extremely pretty child.

"What do you want?" I said.

She showed me. She went straight to my filing cabinet and quickly pulled out the long steel rods that run the length of each drawer, threading through the holes of the cardboard dividers. I don't know how she knew they pulled out, or how she did it so quickly, before I could move, but she got it done.

While I was trying to work the rods back through the dividers she got to the telephone on my desk. It is a pushbutton model, easily operated, and I reached her just before she completed what I suppose could have been a call to Moscow. While I was hanging up the phone she took two steps to the file and pulled out the rod I had just put back. I caught her hand as it was going for the second one.

"No," I barked.

I dropped her hand and it flew to the rod. I grabbed it and gave it a whack. I don't believe in corporal punishment for children, but when they aren't old enough to understand simple English you have to get the message to them somehow.

"No-no," she said, revealing a larger vocabulary than I had given her credit for.

"Right," I said amiably, relieved that we spoke the same language. "No-no."

I led her out of my study and turned her over to my wife. "You'll have to keep her out of there," I said. "She's driving me crazy."

I was back in a fragile soap bubble of concentration when the doors flew open. My granddaughter lurched inside. The bubble burst. "Pompom!" she shrieked.

We took her home Sunday night. I was ready to trade back.

"How's Pugsley?" I asked my daughter-in-law.

"He's fine," she said.

"He's not too much for you?"

"Not so far."

Unfortunately, her baby was early, and we had to take Pugsley back before the pool was finished.

To this day I don't know which is more exasperating—an Airedale or a granddaughter.

30

In this high-tech age it is not surprising to find that our armed forces want recruits who have the capacity to absorb a "sophisticated training program"—but is this more important than such old-fashioned qualities as strength, stamina and courage?

From their effective recruiting slogan, we know that the Marines are still "looking for a few good men," a phrase that may be ambiguous but no doubt sets up vibrations in men who have the right stuff and know it. Besides, the newspaper pictures of Marines fighting here and there in the streets, and being airlifted home on stretchers or in caskets, make it clear what kind of work is expected of a good man in the corps.

In their television and newspaper ads, the other armed forces concentrate on opportunities for military careers in the technology of modern electronic weaponry, perhaps leading to later careers in civilian life. This approach might easily foster the misapprehension that the armed forces no longer care about the kind of stuff that John Wayne personified in fifty movies, from Davey Crockett to Bull Halsey; all they want is whiz kids who got computers for Christmas when they were six years old.

So I find it reassuring that the armed forces are still interested in recruiting individuals who possess such qualities as aggressiveness, protectiveness, confidence, and stability.

I have evidence of this in a letter received by Linda C. Countryman from the Department of Defense Dog Center, Headquarters San Antonio Air Logistics Center, Lackland Air Force Base, Texas.

Ms. Countryman is bookkeeper of Saint James Episcopal Church parish, and the letter to her was sent to me, with her permission, by Father Robert Brown of that church.

> Dear Ms. Countryman:
> Evaluation of your dog has been completed. Unfortunately, your dog does not meet the temperament criteria we have established for prospective military working dogs. Your dog was disqualified for under-aggressiveness.
>
> As you probably know, we only accept dogs which have the capability to complete our sophisticated training programs. A dog must possess a stable temperament which includes an acceptable degree of aggres-

siveness, confidence and protectiveness, and is not too playful, shy, timid, nervous, oversensitive to strangers, or afraid of loud noises (gunfire). A stable temperament is required to insure success in training a dog for use as a multipurpose working dog.

We wish to express our appreciation for your interest in the Department of Defense Military Working Dog Program and sincerely regret that your dog does not qualify. Should you have another dog to offer for evaluation and acceptance, please contact us. Our need to acquire qualified dogs from individual owners is a continuing matter.

It was signed "H. V. Kerker, Chief, Logistics Function, DOD Dog Center."

In a note to me Father Brown said, "Ms. Countryman suggested that the qualities of a military working dog—as described herein—are those of a good husband, as well. . . ."

I wondered whether Ms. Countryman already had a husband with such qualities, or was looking for one. Also, I wondered about her dog.

I was lucky enough to get her on the telephone through Father Brown's office, and found her good-humored about it.

The dog is a German shepherd-Malamute; a stray that Ms. Countryman had taken in. Her name is Missy. Ms. Countryman read about the Department of Defense dog program in "Dear Abby's" advice column and wrote to the center. She received an answer asking her to fill out an application describing her dog and enclosing a photograph of it, which she did.

She then received a letter instructing her to send Missy to the dog center at Lackland, by air, at the Department of Defense's expense. The DOD sent a crate for Missy. Ms. Countryman followed instructions and Missy was sent off to San Antonio, doubtless as nervous as any recruit going away from home for the first time.

A few weeks later the letter which you have just read arrived, indicating that Missy hadn't met the test, and the DOD said they would send her back, by air, if Ms. Countryman preferred it. She said yes, by air, and in time the dog arrived at the airport, a failure, like the washed out college kid in the computer commercial on TV.

Ms. Countryman said she liked Missy, even if she wasn't aggressive enough for the Department of Defense, but she would still like to find a good home for her.

"She walks all over my roof," she said. "It's about a ninety-degree slant, and two stories high. The picture I sent the army showed her up there. She's cost me three hundred dollars for roof repairs."

I asked Ms. Countryman if she had ever been married. "Twice," she said, without amplification.

I assume that neither of her spouses quite came up to the criteria established by the Department of Defense for military working dogs; but that is hardly remarkable, since few men would.

I pointed this out to Ms. Countryman, suggesting that if she were really looking for such a man, he might be hard to find.

"Do you know anyone?" she asked.

I thought of myself; but of course I wasn't eligible.

Besides, I couldn't have passed the test either.

The affluent society is good to its pets, sometimes to the point of absurdity.

Like their owners, many dogs live the good life. They wear tailored clothes, have perfumed baths and patronize beauty shops. More dog food is sold in America than baby food, though this should not surprise anyone who has tasted both. Dogs even travel by air, and go on vacations to Florida.

Consider the adventure of Cleo, a small beagle owned by the daughter of a couple named Andrews. I was reminded of it by the story of Missy and her goose chase to Texas.

When the daughter moved from Southern California to Florida some years ago, Cleo was left behind temporarily, to be flown to the new home after her mistress settled in. Meanwhile, she was lodged in a commercial kennel with every human convenience, including a resident veterinarian and, for all I know, a psychiatrist.

Cleo was to be kept at the kennel until the day she was to fly to Florida. On that day, Andrews was to pick up the beagle at the kennel and drive her to the airport. As a routine precaution, the resident vet had given Cleo a tranquilizer, to keep her from becoming flighty on the trip.

"The dog greeted my husband with gleeful howls," Mrs. Andrews told me. "She went gaily to the car and barked all the way to the airport, trying to get into his lap."

Cleo was anything but tranquil, Andrews thought. But the vet had assured him, "Mr. Andrews, the shot I gave that dog will have the effect of five martinis."

Cleo acted more like a beagle with one martini—a bit exhilarated, a bit uninhibited, but hardly smashed. Andrews put her on a jet airliner, said good-by and went home to his own tranquilizer.

At 6:30 that evening the phone rang in the Andrews home. It was the kennel vet.

"Mrs. Andrews? I have just had a call from your daughter, in Florida."

Mrs. Andrews gasped. "What's wrong!" she cried, fearing that Cleo had met with some misfortune, perhaps fatal.

"Please don't be upset," said the doctor in his most soothing professional tone. "Unfortunately, however, I must tell you that we gave Mr. Andrews, uh, the wrong beagle. Cleo is still here."

The following afternoon the phone rang again. It was the airport. They had a beagle, they told Mr. Andrews, that had been shipped to him, collect, from Florida.

In time, Andrews, the kennel, the airline and providence got matters straightened out. The wrong beagle, whose name is not known to me, was picked up at the airport and driven back to the kennel, sober as an owl. Cleo, properly tranquilized, was taken to the airport at last and flew to Florida in a five-martini blur.

What bemused Mrs. Andrews, however, was the thought that the other beagle, who had presumably led a sheltered life, had flown all the way to Florida and back on one mad escapade, and her owners never even knew she wasn't safe in her kennel.

Anyone who owns a dog in the city has to learn how to deal with bureaucracy, and one of the many frustrations is in not knowing which bureau to call on for help or advice in an emergency. Most of us know whether to phone the police or the sheriff, though even for this basic service there is much blurring of jurisdictions in a metropolis like Los Angeles.

I had lunch one day with a friend, Jean Holloway the television writer, who told me about a recent occurrence in which she tried to get help, or at least advice, from the appropriate agency, with less than gratifying results.

She lives in a part of the Santa Monica Mountains that still provides a rustic habitat for wildlife, despite the encroachment of the city. She has seen deer and heard coyotes and encountered the large birds and smaller mammals that happily survive in this precarious environment.

She also owns a schnauzer, which is a small gray terrier of German origin. Though of feisty disposition, like most terriers, the schnauzer is too small (twelve to fifteen pounds) to give much account of himself in a fight, and in the face of the unknown has no more courage, I would guess, than the rest of us.

What happened was this: The schnauzer was attacked from the rear by a very large bird which my friend, not knowing birds, took for a hawk. "He was huge," she said, spreading her hands as far apart as she could. "He had a wingspread like this. Oh, no—wider than that!"

She is not a large woman, but I would estimate the distance between her outspread hands as between four and five feet. True, the red-tailed hawk is said to have a spread of four feet or more, but a red-tail with a wingspread greater than five feet would be an extraordinary specimen indeed. I am more inclined to think that the bird which attacked her schnauzer was a condor.

"What exactly did the bird do?" I asked.

"It grabbed my schnauzer from behind in its claws, like this," she said, forming her hands into claws to demonstrate that the bird had grasped the dog by his hindquarters.

"What did you do?"

First, she had run out screaming to drive off the bird and rescue the dog. However, the bird did not exactly flee, but merely flapped off to a nearby perch, from which it obviously was planning to renew its attack when the schnauzer's mistress was out of the way.

My friend is not without experience in the bureaucratic labyrinth, but even *she* didn't think at first to call the State Department of Fish and Game, which turned out to be the appropriate bureau. I was not taking notes, and cannot retrace the series of inquiries by which she finally arrived at that department and found the right man in the right niche.

She told him what had happened and the man asked her to describe the bird, which she did as best she could, not being able to demonstrate the wing-spread by extending her arms over the telephone.

"What did he say?" I asked.

"He said, 'Lady—did you harm that bird? That bird is protected.'"

She said she told the man she meant no harm to the bird, but had every reason to believe that the bird meant to harm her schnauzer.

"I told him I'd never seen anything like it," she said, "and asked him just what he thought the bird would have done. He said schnauzers are small and gray and look like a rabbit, and the bird thought my schnauzer was a rabbit. He said the bird would have lifted him and flown up and dropped him from a height to stun him, and would then have torn him to pieces."

She told the man she didn't mind the bird being protected, but what she wanted to know was, who was going to protect her schnauzer.

"He said, 'Lady—the schnauzer has you—the bird has us.'"

I reminded her that the condor was in very grave danger of becoming extinct. There were only fifty of them left, if that many, and if they were to survive they had to have protection.

She understood that, but she was still uneasy about her schnauzer.

31

It was going to be a leisurely Sunday morning and I was sitting in my swivel rocker by the window, having my second cup of coffee and going through the paper, when Denny came in from outdoors.

"Everything seems to be happening," she said. "George's cats are out in force."

"Is that all?"

"Well, it's just sort of . . . exciting. You ought to come out and have a look."

She is always trying to get me outdoors, as if I can't appreciate it from looking through the window.

"The more of George's cats we have," I said, "the fewer gophers you will have."

"I hope that's true"

It was odd about George and his cats. They weren't really his cats. They were neighborhood wild cats. Domestic cats gone feral. They were nobody's cats. They couldn't be touched. But George fed them, and we called them George's cats. We were to learn before long that they were our cats, too.

Denny went back outdoors and I went back to my paper. She came back inside with more news.

"We have four scrub jays," she said.

That was curious. Usually we had only two. They were very protective of their territory.

"You probably saw two twice," I said.

"No, I saw four all at once."

I wondered what it meant.

"If you happen to get up for anything," she said, "maybe you can just look out the window, see my tulips. They're blooming at last."

When I got up to go into the kitchen for another cup of coffee, I walked over to the windows looking out on the garden. She had planted the tulips just beyond the brick stoop so they could easily be seen from inside the house. They were of several colors—red, yellow, white, vermillion, and that pale greenish-yellow. They were full-bodied, opulent, velvet in texture, and voluptuously open.

I had always regarded tulips with disbelief. They seemed slightly overblown, as if perhaps they were from some master painter's early work, before his eye and his skill matured. These were vivid and exuberant, and I felt a sudden lift of spirits, as I sometimes do when I switch stations on my car radio, turning off the news, and catch a strain of Mozart or Vivaldi.

I looked out at the yard. Our slender young eucalyptus and the young jacaranda, and the old pepper tree and its offspring shone silver in the bright morning light.

The Airedale was out in the yard, trotting about, tail up, rediscovering his territory. There was a dove in the bird feeder that hangs from the patio cover. A scrub jay was parked on top of the playhouse down on the lower level, revving up, no doubt, to attack the dove and seize the feeder. The new Bermuda lawn around the playhouse was pitted by gopher holes. One of George's cats, black and glossy as a spider, was in a patient crouch. Good cat. I had a feeling that everything was in equilibrium.

The pool was clean and blue. In its setting of walls and terraces it had that timeless, placeless look of a Maxfield Parrish painting. I walked around the deck and came upon a regiment of ants devouring the carcass of a yellowjacket.

The yellowjacket is the most striking of our wasps, so aptly named for its dazzling yellow and jet-black jacket. In flight it has the acrobatic skill and menacing whine of its species, and of course it is armed. Usually we leave the yellowjacket alone, not wanting to make it angry and provoke it to sting. It has few enemies, if any.

Yet here it lay, rapidly being eaten away by ants that came relentlessly across the pool deck in a column ten feet long. Soon there would be nothing left but its black and yellow armor. I was reminded of that mystery of World War II in which some caravan of Bedouins crossing the trackless Sahara, years after the war, came upon a solitary airplane, apparently intact, with fuel left in its tanks, and no sign of its crew—not even bones.

How had the wasp died? Who or what had shot it down? How had the ant scout found it? How had he reported this intelligence to his captains? How had they given the order to march; and how had the column of soldiers found their way back to the prize?

But of course all this is kid stuff. I'm sure I knew all the answers when I was a small boy. I would spend many hours observing such mysterious events in the field, and then go to the library to look them up.

I wonder if kids these days waste their time on such field studies and philosophical speculations. I have an idea my first thoughts about life and death and the hereafter and the meaning of things were inspired by such backyard tragedies—a caterpillar stung by a wasp, a worm snatched by a bird, a lizard carried off by a cat, and in the end, everything devoured by the ants.

I remember finding the skeleton of a bird, or a tiny mammal, or a mummified lizard, and concluding that death was permanent. In half a century, I have seen no evidence to the contrary.

Though I had no desire to intrude on the yellowjacket's piecemeal consumption by the ants, since it was obviously in God's order of things, and doubtless a good idea, I didn't want it to be happening on my pool deck. I got a broom and a dustpan and swept up the carcass and put it in the trash, then got our can of Raid and Raided the ant column, like a German Stuka machine-gunning an Allied column on a long straight road in France.

While engaged in this omnipotent and amoral act, I thought of what I had read in the paper a day or two earlier about today's children spending their afternoons and Saturdays in air-conditioned shopping malls playing video games.

"What to do with kids," said a USC professor, commenting on this phenomenon, "has been a problem since they became free from farm chores in recent times. They used to hang out on street corners, but now there is no action on street corners anymore, or more likely, there is a mall where there used to be a street corner. . . ."

But I don't mean to condemn shopping malls, some of which I like, nor to moralize about video games, which are the ultimate toy for our times.

I'm just wondering whether children who never have any time to spend in their backyards, alone, thinking about butterflies and lizards and beetles and spiders and scrub jays, aren't missing something of value. In our backyard alone there are thousands of insects and scores of species, and each is equipped for battle—armor, weapons, wile or camouflage—each is in danger of instant death. It is constant, savage, unrelenting warfare. And we can watch it, and think about it, and intercede, if we have a mind to, with our God-like power.

I found a very small lizard in the spa. He was alive; the water line was low and he was clinging to the plaster just below the tile, which evidently was too slippery to climb. I knew he would never get out. I got the net and fished him up and dropped him in the garden. I wondered how many insects he would get before one of George's cats got him.

I went back into the house to get another cup of coffee and read the paper. I had saved a lizard's life and destroyed a thousand ants. I wondered how that morning's work would look in my ledger.

32

It is not often that my wife asks me to call on my hunting instincts and play the protector, but one spring morning I realized that she wanted me to do something about her gopher.

We had always had gophers, and usually she let them have their minor triumphs. But that year she had a lovely stand of tulips, and it infuriated her to find them toppled, one after another, by her rarely seen foe.

I knew my help was being solicited when she came into the house and said, "Damn that gopher. He's getting my tulips."

Late in the previous fall, on my advice, she had planted daffodils. I had gotten the idea from Dalton. He told me gophers wouldn't touch a tulip bed if daffodils were planted in it; he had also suggested dropping lighted safety flares down the gopher's holes. "Burns up their oxygen," he explained.

"You think it will work?" Denny asked.

"What, the daffodils?"

"No, the flares."

"Let's try the daffodils first," I said.

She had planted daffodils. I kept safety flares in the back of my car, but in all the years I had carried them I had never had to use one, and I didn't care to. I have never liked any kind of fireworks or explosives.

Now it was spring, the tulips were up, and the daffodils weren't doing the job. I didn't really have any sense of engagement with the gopher until that afternoon, after Denny had left the house to attend a birthday party. I was in the kitchen, idly looking out the window, when I saw him.

He popped up out of a hole in the tulip bed, just off the patio. Only his head and shoulders showed. His eyes were bright and alert. He swiveled his head about in jerks, like a mechanical toy, surveying all 360 degrees of the surrounding yard. I felt that surge of adrenalin; an instinctive reaction a billion years old. My pulse raced; muscles tensed for action.

I suppose he was part of the equation himself; but I felt no compassion for him. I saw him only as arrogant, greedy, destructive, lawless—the embodiment of evil.

"I saw your gopher," I told Denny when she came home.

"You did!" There was loathing in her voice, but excitement, too. I realized she was caught in woman's age-old dilemma—the choice between her compassion for all living things and her ferocity against any threat to her nest.

"I'll buy a gun," I said. It was a schoolboy threat of mine that was never carried out.

"No," she said. "You'll shoot one of the neighbors."

More likely, I thought, I'd shoot myself in the foot.

I had already forgotten about buying the gun the next day when I came home and found the canary in a rusty old bird cage in the kitchen. The bird was pale yellow, with touches of orange. Denny had never owned a bird in her life. I had never thought of her as the kind of woman who would keep a bird for a pet, going "tweet-tweet" and all that.

"Where'd you get the canary?" I asked.

She and the now-and-then gardener, Jim, had found it flapping about in the yard, evidently lost and bewildered. Between them they had easily caught it. There were hundreds like that around the city. Either they had escaped from their cages, or been cruelly put out by callous owners who had tired of them; the birds were unable to cope with life outdoors.

"Where'd you get that cage?" I asked.

It was one some children had thrown into our backyard years before, and Denny had put it down in the garage with the rest of the junk, knowing, I suppose, that someday a canary would turn up.

"It won't live," I said.

It chirped that high, piping, fragmentary sound canaries make.

"Tweet-tweet!" Denny answered.

"Oh, no," I sighed.

She gave the bird some of my wild birdseed, hung a bauble in the cage for the bird to play with and put the cage in her bathroom, just off the bedroom, for the night.

The next morning after the clock radio went on I heard it chirping. Denny got up and looked into the bathroom.

"Hi, tweetie," she said. "Good morning."

The bird chirped.

"You hear that?" she said. "It answered me."

The pendulum had swung toward compassion for all creatures, great and small.

It would swing back, I knew, when the gopher got another tulip.

The bird seemed happy from the start. Day by day its song grew more exuberant. Besides chirping, it took to rattling its cage, like a gorilla, and scattering its seeds and grits on the tile floor.

It is my custom to take a short nap in midafternoon, after which, refreshed, I pitch into my work. But I found that a chirping canary murders sleep. There is an irregular rhythm to it, full of fits and starts and exasperating silences, and waiting for the next cadenza is as bad as hearing it.

Because of the bird, I took to the couch in my study for my nap. From the beginning, though, Denny was discontented with the bird cage because it wasn't gold. She had preceded the Women's Liberation Movement long enough that she grew up singing that poignant ballad, "She's Only a Bird in a Gilded Cage," and now that she had a bird it didn't seem right for it not to have a gilded cage.

Actually, though it kept me from sleeping, I didn't resent the bird at all, and gave it my support. One day when Denny was at work I dropped in at Hal's Pet Shop to see if they had a book on how to raise a canary. It was something we knew absolutely nothing about.

The young woman showed me a book on canaries for $14.95.

"We don't want to know that much about canaries," I said. "Don't you have anything cheaper?"

She found a small paperback that was only 49¢. "That's good enough," I said.

"You can have it for nothing," she said. "It looks a bit weatherbeaten."

I also bought some seed and some grits or whatever they're called—those hard little stones that canaries need for their craws, whatever craws are.

Hal also had a gilded bird cage, but I didn't presume to buy a cage that my wife hadn't seen. I had had no experience in bird cages, and didn't want to get the bird off to a bad start. I didn't even ask the price. But I told her about it and the next Saturday morning she went to look at it. She must have liked it. She brought it home, along with a sack full of what they evidently call "furniture," including a bathtub.

"How much did it cost?" I asked.

"You mean the cage itself?"

"Yes, to start with."

"The cage was forty-nine ninety-five."

I thought it over and realized that forty-nine ninety-five was very close to fifty dollars and I would have said the bird cage cost fifty dollars. But certain women, I had noticed, beginning with my mother, were given to quoting the prices of things to the penny, evidently deluding themselves that ninety-nine cents was substantially cheaper than a dollar.

So, I realized, we had bought a fifty dollar bird cage for a tramp canary, plus incidentals.

I knew that was only the beginning. The bird would get sick, sooner or later, and run up an enormous medical bill. When we left the house for a weekend or on vacation it would have to be boarded out, and possibly would pine away.

Meanwhile, Mozart had taken up a vigil in the bathroom under the cage, and the house was full of tension.

Denny went out one Saturday morning before Mother's Day to buy presents for our two daughters-in-law, and I decided it was a good time for me to get the present I had in mind for her and sneak it into the house.

I wanted to get her a male canary to go with Tweetie (for that indeed had become the bird's name). I wouldn't have dared to buy her a bird, except that she had shown a surprising affection for the foundling, and had said maybe she should get another one so it would have some company.

Of course we didn't really know whether it was a male or female, but according to our 49¢ canary book, and all the expert counsel we had received from friends and strangers, it was probably a female because it merely chirped and twittered instead of singing. That's why she called it Tweetie.

On the other hand, from what the woman on Hal's answering service had told me, and the rather ambiguous explanation I'd got from Dr. Schreiber for my friend Work about his parakeet, I didn't have any confidence in that conclusion.

After Denny left the house I drove to Hal's and asked to see a male he had told me about on the phone. It turned out to be an unusual looking canary—pale yellow with a light gray-brown head, collar and wings. It looked as if it might have a sparrow in its family tree. It was in a sullen mood and wouldn't sing for me, but Hal said it was a good singer, with a low voice, soft and sweet.

"Can we put him in the same cage with the other one?" I asked. I didn't especially care to buy another fifty dollar cage.

"No problem, if the other one's a female."

"We're not really sure."

"Why don't you bring it in, and we'll find out."

"You can tell?"

"Sure, most of the time."

I went home to get the bird. I was going to take it to the pet shop in its cage, but the cage was nearly three feet high, and I would have had to carry it in the passenger seat and fasten the seat belt around it to keep it from tipping into the windshield. It seemed foolish.

Then I remembered the old bird cage down in the garage, the one my wife had used as a temporary house for the canary. I brought it up and caught the bird, somewhat to my surprise, and put it in the old and smaller cage and took it to the pet shop. Hal caught it easily and took it out of the cage and began to examine it minutely.

"This bird is five years old," he said.

"How can you tell?"

"See that 75 on this leg band? That's its birth-date." Evidently its breeder had put the band on and it had never been taken off.

"Is five years very old?"

"It's old for a bird."

He pursed his lips and blew the bird's feather away from what he wanted to see. "I'm afraid it's a male," he said. "But there's one way to be sure. We can put it in the cage with that male, and if the male doesn't attack it, we're pretty sure it's a fe-male."

He put Tweetie in with the male. We waited. The male was on a high perch. My wife's bird sat uneasily on a lower one. Nothing happened, but there was a great deal of tension. Suddenly the male dropped down to the lower perch and sat beside Tweetie. But he made no hostile move.

"Hmm," Hal said. "Maybe it *is* a female."

Then—zap!—he struck, beak snapping. Fierce and sudden.

"Nope," Hal said. "You've got a male there."

But he said it would work out all right if we kept them in separate cages. When males were separated they sometimes sang to each other. The bottom of the old cage in which I had brought Tweetie to the store was falling out and the gates were loose so he lent me a cage to take the new bird home in, and put Tweetie in a cardboard box. I put the old cage in the passenger seat and the new cage and the box on the back seat and drove them home.

I put Tweetie back in her cage and put the borrowed cage with the new bird in it in my study. He gave a cheep. "Keep your mouth shut," I told him. "You're supposed to be a secret."

I went out and shut the double doors behind me. When my wife came home she started wrapping the presents she had bought for our daughters-in-law. Once or twice I went into my study and tried to intimidate the bird with scowls and threatening gestures, hoping to keep him quiet. When I came out I shut the doors again.

"Is there something in there you don't want me to see?" Denny asked.

"Yes," I said, knowing it would be better to admit that much. At least it would keep her out.

My tactics must have worked, because the bird was silent until we both changed and were leaving the house to go out for the evening. When I opened the car door I realized I had blown it. I had left the old bird cage in the passenger seat. She opened the door and stood there, looking down at the battered old cage.

"What is this?" she said.

"Well," I said. "It seems to be a bird cage."

On Mother's Day the new bird awakened us at dawn with a lovely serenade—low, soft, sweet and melodious.

Denny was enchanted. Of course we had to buy the other fifty dollar cage.

33

Occasionally someone who reads something I have written about dogs or cats, or even snakes or mice, deduces from it that I am "insensitive" to animals, and ought not to have any pets.

Of course I am not insensitive to animals, but perhaps I am not close to my pets in the same way they are close to theirs. I am not emotionally dependent on them, though my feelings for them often run deeper than even I suspect at the time. I tend to be reticent about my feelings, for animals and people too. It is a legacy, perhaps, from my dour forebears.

I am fascinated by animals, tame or wild. I am attracted by their beauty, their grace, their superhuman skills; and I especially admire those wild creatures that survive within our cities, subtly adapting their instincts while clinging to their devastated habitats.

That is why I put out feeders for wild birds. They take what they want, and it might seem that they give nothing back, except their cautious presence: our doves, our jays, our finches and our mockingbirds, and the occasional exotics whose names I am not sure of. Our relationship is tentative. None has ever approached me with what might have been taken as an offering of friendship, or an overture to closer acquaintance. They remain exquisitely wary of me, but they give me what I want of them, without knowing it. They entertain me. They are my circus. They also are my ballet. And they help to remind me that we are not the only species on earth.

But I know that pets need something more from us than provender and protection. People who cannot enter into some higher kind of bond with pets ought not to have them, I suppose.

I think my wife's feeling about pets is much like mine, or appears to be on the surface. She had no pets as a child, and has not always cared for them by the book, but they have never seemed to love her the less for that. She can do no wrong. They adore her. She has a rapport with animals that used to baffle me, but which I long ago accepted.

So I was only slightly surprised that spring when she caught the fallen canary on the ground in the backyard and took it in; and when it disappointed her by being a poor singer, as I have already recounted, I bought her another one that sang like Enrico Caruso.

She cared for both of them, doing all the dirty little housekeeping chores with uncomplaining good humor. When the new bird stopped singing the first summer we had him, we were assured that he was only molting and would sing again come fall. Fall came and he did not sing. But Denny bore this disappointment with patience, whistling and cooing at him every morning as if she could inspire him to sing again.

Meanwhile, during this affair, I began to notice the deterioration of Jolie. She had been a runt to begin with, was never very vigorous, and now she was more than thirteen years old. She had begun to lose her senses and was no longer able to cope with the Airedale, who was always gentle but too playful for her, and the Yorkie, who was feisty and sometimes mean. Fluff followed Pugsley like his Secret Service bodyguard, and was jealous of any other dog he looked at.

Finally Jolie became blind and deaf, and bent by arthritis, and did nothing but bump into things or stand in a heap, whimpering. "I don't think she's getting anything out of life," Denny said one day.

The next morning I took the dog down to the animal hospital and Dr. Morehouse, who has doctored our pets for thirty years, agreed.

I fed the other dogs for two or three days but ignored the pan the poodle had eaten out of. Finally I brought it into the kitchen and put it in the sink. Later Denny went into the kitchen and came out looking tearful.

"Seeing Jolie's pan," she said. "It got me."

"No use feeling guilty," I said. "She was old and miserable."

"I know."

The next Sunday morning I was reading the paper and Denny went into her bathroom and I heard her give an odd little cry. She usually talked to her birds, but I sensed an anguished note.

She came out. "Tweetie's dead," she said.

"He was an old bird," I reminded her.

"Yes."

Later she carried the cage out and put it on the back porch. Tweetie lay on the bottom of it on his back.

"Do you want me to do it?" I asked her.

"No, I'll do it."

It was a year of attrition.

We weren't sure. We thought Mozart was about thirteen, maybe fourteen years old. But she was a good, healthy, alert cat, showing no signs of senility, and seemed to have a lot of life ahead.

I wasn't worried about her. I had an idea she was sustained by a sinister ambition—to outlive me. On the other hand, she had grown sweeter to me. I took it as a sign that I must have mellowed.

A few weeks later Denny left the house to drive to work and heard a cat crying under her car. It was Mozart. She was unable to move. Evidently she had been hit by a car.

That ever-present urban hazard, which in her street-smart way she had eluded for thirteen years, had finally ended her career.

Denny realized that Mozart couldn't walk; couldn't stand up. She picked her up and drove her straight down the hill to the hospital. Dr. Morehouse was on duty early, as usual, to tend the casualties of the night. He quickly found that Mozart could not be saved.

Whatever my relations with her had been, whatever my shortcomings as her owner and keeper (if a cat can be said to have an owner and a keeper), I felt something close to grief, and I knew I would miss her. She had played a role in many of my small adventures, and her character was never anything but what a cat's should be. Though we had always been tentative with each other, not to say wary, and at times surly, our relationship was not without mutual respect and reward, and I have an idea that she would have missed me too, in some vague way, without thinking about it.

She had a good life for a cat. We had denied her whatever rewards there might be for a cat in motherhood, so as not to repeat the errors of our past. Two litters—one Shaggy's, one Gato's—was enough for us in our lifetime. I am not sure that Mozart wouldn't have liked one set of kittens, but it is a numbers game. There are too many cats in the world already.

She was a tough and active cat and, I suspect, she was at least as happy as those fat, pampered, inside cats that spend their lives dozing in a warm window on a satin pillow.

Like all our animals except my wife's canaries, she was kept outdoors most of the time, inured to the elements for which her genes and evolution had fitted her. Of course she came in every morning when I went out to get the paper, and she generally had the run of the house during the day. But at night, unless we forgot it, she was put out again, in fair weather and foul, so that she would not forget that she was, after all, a creature of the wild, and not be softened by an artificial life indoors, looking wistfully out the window, like so many cats I have seen.

Outside at night she was able to enjoy the scents of the neighborhood; the calls and lamentations of her own species; the hooting of owls; the quick furtive movements of nocturnal things; the magic of full moons. She had her adventures, though of course they were somewhat circumscribed by the fact that she was a spayed female; but she made calls and had her secret places. She was of course free. Even so, she knew where home was, and the only time she would be missing for more than a day or so would be when one of us inadvertently locked her in the garage.

Though she might be friendly with visitors, she rarely jumped up on my lap, and she mewed about my ankles only when my wife was gone and she knew she would have to look to me for food. Though I never tried to win her affection with false blandishments, I was civil to her, and often spoke with her when we were alone. Cats are good company for men who otherwise would talk to themselves.

"Well, cat," I would sometimes say as I scanned the paper, "the Dodgers blew another one in the top of the ninth."

Of course it was gibberish to her, but she listened, and sometimes responded by walking past my ankles and brushing me with her whiskers, since she had no tail.

Sometimes, on the other hand, I would try to pick her up and she would rebuff my overture with a hiss. I took that as a sign that she wanted space, a wish that I respected.

We had been rather seriously at odds when both of us were younger. Now and then, from the feathers scattered about our fountain, I knew that she had gotten a bird. Having put out the seed that brought them into harm's way, I felt responsible when one of the birds was picked off. But early on I withdrew from that equation. There had been something comical and vain about my attempt to intercede, beyond hanging the feeders above the reach of a leaping cat.

Time finally took away the cat's advantage as it was taking away mine.

Until the end she was still able to make the stealthy approach, but her marvelous timing was just infinitesimally off in the sudden, silent pounce, the swift stroke of tooth and claw. We both grew creaky, like two old gladiators retired from the arena.

Sometimes I miss her still.

34

It was not long after Mozart left us that Denny came home one day with a cockatiel. She went down to the garage and brought up Tweetie's cage and installed the new resident in it.

I was astonished. The cockatiel is a small, crested Australian parrot, and like all parrots it is noisy, dirty and mean. Males and females look alike. It is a wild bird, only recently out of the jungle. She might as well have brought home a cassowary.

Her cockatiel was a soft gray and white, with a yellow-green crest like a Trojan warrior's helmet, and large orange spots on its cheeks, like the rouge spots on gaudy women. Altogether it gave an impression of decadent anarchy and arrogance— the kind of bird one might find in a German Expressionist painting; a bird created not by nature but by a disturbed imagination.

It didn't sing. It whistled, not to say screeched. If a bird is happy in direct ratio with the amount of noise it makes, this was a happy bird. It could whistle nonstop for half an hour, never making anything close to a melody.

The irony of it was that Denny didn't really know how happy the bird was. She was away at work all day, while I was often at home, trying to work, so she missed the concerts. By the time she came home the bird was exhausted from its efforts, and simply signed off for the day with an atonal cadenza or two, and a rude demand for attention.

Denny evidently loved this creature, which she rather appropriately called Pooh-Bah, after the pompous Lord High Everything Else in *The Mikado,* and tried to teach it to talk. She started with "Hello," a simple enough beginning. Every morning, while she was in the bathroom, she kept calling to it: "Hel-oh-o! . . . Hel-oh-o! . . . Hel-oh-o! . . ."

It never learned to say "Hello," or anyway it declined to. It simply sat dumb through its lesson. I think the bird was just too mean to do what Denny wanted it to do. I think it could talk all right, because one day when I was home alone, trying to take a nap, it kept saying "Big deal! . . . Big deal!"

Last summer when Denny went to France for the wedding of our daughter-in-law's sister, she left the cockatiel in my care, and I had a terrible incident with it.

Besides his seed he had to be given fresh bath water every day and a leaf of lettuce. I opened the door of his cage to get the bath out and the bird flew out the opening. He flew straight across Denny's bathroom, through vines and potted trees, no doubt thinking he was free in a jungle, and crashed into the glass wall and fell into her sunken tub, where he flopped about, skidding on the tiles and screaming bloody murder.

I was after him, my curses mixing with his. I lowered myself into the tub and tried to catch him. This was my only chance. If he got out of the tub he'd kill himself crashing into walls. I knew my wife had some strange affection for this brute, and I didn't want his death on my conscience.

I got both hands on him, but one wing and his head were free. He flapped the free wing, shrieking, then got my left forefinger in his beak. I couldn't free my finger without losing my hold. He let me go, evidently to find a meatier target. He bit me on the ball of the thumb, holding on fiercely, grinding his jaws. The skin turned blue; blood oozed out. I yanked my hand free. He bit me on the forefinger of my other hand.

It isn't easy to get out of a three-foot-deep tub without using your hands. I crawled out on my knees and elbows, the bird still flapping in my hands, still with a death grip on my finger. I lurched to the cage, stuffed him in, wrenched my right hand from his beak and slammed the door.

I had bloody wounds in five places.

He got on his perch and glared at me, breathing hard, like a prizefighter at the end of the eighth round. I glared at him, breathing hard.

"Big deal!" he croaked.

Sometimes when I was home alone and the bird was whistling, I would think of my friend Gomez and his parrot, down at his little store by the beach in Baja. Gomez had bought a parrot and tried to teach it to talk, for companionship; but the parrot was reluctant, and Gomez said that if it didn't talk, he was going to cook it. I don't know what happened but I do know that the next time I went down to see Gomez the parrot was gone.

As I say, sometimes when I was home alone and the cockatiel was whistling, I would find myself wondering how Gomez would handle it.

One year we were visited by some birds that are much more common than cockatiels, at least in the civilized world, but I considered them just as troublesome, in their way.

I had noticed only a few at first, probably scouts, but their numbers grew until they seemed to be in control of the air over our backyard. All my crude attempts to discourage them failed, and finally I turned to Ralph Schreiber, the county ornithologist, for help. Instead of just giving him a ring, I decided to write:

Dear Ralph:
I am making this an open letter because I have an idea that my problem is not unique, and if you can help me, your answer might also help others on Mt. Washington and the nearby hills.

We have had a lively spring. I don't think we ever had more birds at our feeder, including a few species that we had never seen in our backyard before. That is part of the problem. One of those species is the pigeon. I thought maybe they were visiting from one of the parks, or just passing through on the way to somewhere else, but they're still here and seem to come by at about the same hours, twice a day, to clean out our feeders.

We do not want pigeons. As you know, they are large, gluttonous and pushy—the slobs of the bird world—and once they have found a home they are very hard to get rid of. For years we had no pigeons. Then, as I remember, I saw one, a loner; next time it was a pair. I drove them off by running outdoors onto the terrace and waving my arms and shouting insults. These demonstrations seemed to discourage them for a time, and I assumed that they had gotten my message and wouldn't be back.

Evidently they had only gone off to get their friends. Soon I realized that they were coming in ever larger groups, driving off the smaller birds. My wife was out in the yard working with her flowers all day last Sunday and she said she saw at least a dozen of them at one time.

They have virtually taken over, and have upset the whole ecological picture. It isn't that I don't like pigeons, but I like them in their place. They belong in parks and plazas. What would Trafalgar Square be without its pigeons? Or the Piazza San Marco? Or our own Pershing Square? But they don't do anything for my backyard.

I have considered several lines of action. First I thought of buying a popgun and sitting in my outdoor rocker on the terrace and popping every pigeon that lighted on the feeder. (Nothing lethal; just one of those toys that shoot corks but make a loud pop.) But this would obviously take too much of my time. I could only do it when the weather was nice, and then I'd want to drink beer, to pace the time between pigeons, and of course the more beer I drank, the worse my aim would become.

I also thought of having an electrician rig up an electric horn by the feeder, with a button to push inside the house by my indoor rocker. That way, I could sit there looking out the window and every time a pigeon lighted on the feeder I could give it a blast of the horn. But that, too, would require a lot of my time; besides, the intermittent horn blasts might drive off my wife as well as the pigeons.

I am writing to you to find out if you have any ideas for me. I know you're a pelican man, but I should think you could confer with some of your fellow ornithologists there at the museum and come up with something. The way things are going I wouldn't be surprised if we began to get sea gulls.

And then who knows—pelicans might be next.

Jack Smith

A day or two later I received a telephone call from one of Shreiber's colleagues, Julian Donahue. Donahue isn't in birds; he's the museum's moth man, but he happens to be a neighbor of mine on the hill, and he felt responsible.

He said Shreiber was in Argentina. It was a familiar story. Schreiber was never around when I needed him. Always out investigating pelicans or boobies at some extremity of the earth.

"He's doing some research into the Argentine pelican," Donahue said, confirming my suspicions.

However, being a neighbor, Donahue was just the man for me on the pigeon question. To my surprise, he told me that my pigeons were not the foreign species we have imported to this country and which frequent our parks.

"Do they have a band across their tails?" he asked.

"Well, yes," I said, "I think so."

"Right. They're band-tails."

The band-tailed pigeon, he told me, was a native species *(Columba fasciata)*. They had come down from the mountains and were nesting this season on our hill. Thousands of them had been driven out when the great fires of the previous fall had devastated their habitat. They also had another problem. They were good eating and good hunting (being sporty fliers), and overzealous hunters had almost wiped them out in the nineteenth century.

I was chagrined to find that I had been adding to this noble native's woes by driving them off my property. My campaign against the band-tails was cancelled instantly, and they have been regular and welcome visitors ever since.

I also told Donahue about our wasps. Denny had noticed them one morning as she was leaving for work. She walked out onto the front porch and shut the door and then opened the door and walked back in.

"We have wasps," she said.

There was a colony of them, about the size of a hand, clustered on the wall. Two of them sat apart, poised and alert, like sentries.

"Leave them alone," I said. "Maybe they'll go away."

They didn't go away. They didn't seem to be doing anything, but I was uneasy. Insects are never idle. They are mindless little machines, always running.

Then one morning one of the sentries flew angrily at Denny and lit on her coat.

"You've got to do something," she said. I thought of calling the exterminators, but I didn't want to tamper with the ecology of Mt. Washington. Having Donahue on the phone was a piece of luck.

"Actually," he said, "I'm the moth man. You'd better talk to Roy Snelling. He's our wasp man."

He put Snelling on. From my description, Snelling wasn't sure just what we had.

"There's so doggone many wasps here in Southern California," he said. "If I knew what they were I might be able to say what they're doing. Maybe Donahue can stop by your place on his way home and get me a couple."

That evening we waited eagerly for Donahue to arrive. Finally a yellow station wagon rolled up in front of the house. It had a personalized license plate that said MOTHS. Not much competition for that one, I guessed.

A young man and a young woman hopped out of the wagon, each in safari shorts and armed with a butterfly net. It was certainly among the most enchanting sights I had ever seen on Mt. Washington.

The woman turned out to be Kathy Donahue, Julian's wife and also the museum librarian. She and Donahue looked at the wasp nest and wondered how to get their specimens without getting all of us stung.

"It looks like a one-man job," said Mrs. Donahue.

"I suppose so," Donahue said.

Suddenly a lone wasp flew onto the porch. Mrs. Donahue swished her net expertly. The wasp was caught. Donahue trapped it in a little bottle and in half a minute the wasp was dead.

Donahue looked up at the colony. "I wonder what they'd do," he said, "if I just put my net over the whole bunch,"

He reached the net up and covered the wasps. The sentries flew to the attack. Mrs. Donahue swung her net and caught them neatly. Donahue withdrew his net and the other wasps stayed put.

Mrs. Donahue meanwhile had been examining a number of tiny moths caught in the cobwebs around our porchlight. "You've got a bunch of micros there," she said.

"What are micros?" I asked.

"Microlepidoptera," said Mrs. Donahue.

Donahue peered into the cobwebs. "You've got some diamondbacks there," he said.

The next morning I phoned the museum to find out about the wasps. "What you have," Donahue said, "is *Polistes aurifer,* a common paper wasp."

"What are they up to?" I asked.

"Just as we thought," he said. "They've been dispossessed. They've lost their nest. They're only geared to build nests in the spring, so evidently they're just hanging on. In the fall they'll die."

"What should we do?"

"It might be interesting," he said, "just to watch and see what happens. Not much is known about what wasps do when their nests have been destroyed."

Our hands were tied. We were running a refuge. Not only for homeless band-tailed pigeons, but also for homeless *Polistes aurifers,* not to mention micros and diamondbacks.

At least we could thank God that the diamondbacks weren't rattlesnakes, but merely moths.

35

We missed Mozart more than I would have thought. Sometimes before going to bed I would forget for a moment and wonder whether she was out, and when I came home I would sometimes hesitate for a moment after opening the door, as if expecting her to come hurtling out of the shrubbery to slip indoors, the way she did.

I imagined, though, that we would never acquire another cat. We would probably be traveling more, if only down to our house in Mexico, and cats don't travel well, don't like being enclosed in moving cars.

Then, suddenly, we seemed to have twelve cats. Or was it nine? The count changed every day. Sometimes it was only two or three; sometimes none. They were wild.

I don't mean wildcats or bobcats *(Lynx rufus)*, which are actually found in our nearby mountains, but domestic cats *(Felis catus)* that have gone wild, even though they were born in the city and cling to the neighborhood. Domestic cats that have gone wild are called wild cats (two words) or feral cats (*fera* being the Latin word for wild animals, from *ferus*, meaning fierce).

That is the kind of cats we had. They were the survivors of at least three litters—all, as far as we know, produced by the same female, a calico named Mona.

Her latest litter numbered four, evidently born inside a small grape-stake enclosure around the cooling unit beside our front porch. That's where they were when we discovered them, and whenever we tried to close in on them they would disappear.

As far as we know, it was the first time the calico had had a litter at our house. We don't know what place she had chosen for the earlier ones. When she first turned up in the neighborhood with a litter, a man down the street had disposed of the kittens.

After that our neighbor George, a very humane man who hoped for a different solution, had put out food for her and tried to tame her so he could have her spayed and interrupt the cycle. He named her Mona. But Mona declined domesticity. He never tamed or trapped her.

Unfortunately, the neighborhood's tomcats didn't find Mona that hard to get. The result of her promiscuity was a series of wonderfully variegated litters. I didn't know siblings could be so different. Mona seemed to have flouted Mendelian law, though what she was really doing, I suppose, was proving it.

We were not sure which cats were of the same litter, but among those who came to our door (all apparently Mona's) were an orange one; a mottled tabby that George called Paintrag; a tortoise-shell type with a face dramatically divided between black and buff, which I called Harlequin (Quin for short); and two that looked like pure bred Siamese—even to the startling blue eyes—though there wasn't a chance that they were. George called them Yin and Yang and said Yin was a female and Yang a male, but I don't know how he knew, since he had never had one in hand for a conclusive examination.

We had been aware of these mavericks for months. After they were grown they hunted in our backyard, and often at night they hunkered down under parked cars for shelter, and when we came home we would see their eyes blazing in our head-lights.

But they never came to our door meowing for a handout. We knew George was feeding some of them, out of kindness, and also so he could tame them enough to catch them and have them neu-tered, one by one, so the population explosion could be checked at their generation, if not at Mona's. It was easy enough for us to let George do it.

But then the new litter was born at our door-step, and we saw the kittens every day, tiny but al-ready incredibly quick. We began to put out milk, and then, as the kittens grew, canned cat food. Mona had thrust herself and her brood upon us, which is a cat's way. We had been chosen. The ba-ton had been passed on to us.

At first the kittens came up on the porch only when Mona did. Sometimes one or two would be eating from the dish with their mother, while the others, at the same time, would still be trying to suckle.

They were not a beautiful litter. The father evidently had been a big black tomcat with some white on his neck, and white boots. We'd seen him around. Two of the kittens were marked that way, one with a white blaze down its nose and one with a white bib. The one with the blaze we called Blaze, after that rascal dog of long ago. The other two were a dark brownish-black, somewhat the color of Mozart; one of these was smaller than the others, almost a runt.

In time they would hold their ground at the feeding dish while we moved to within a few feet of it, but if we tried kneeling beside the dish they turned and scampered into the shrubs that concealed their hideaway. We began leaving the door open and standing out of sight. Tentatively, one or two would creep into the house. Soon all began to enter and explore. But if we took a step or made a sound they fled, jostling each other as they hustled out the doorway.

How wild they really were was demonstrated for us one morning when Denny inched up quietly behind one of the kittens as it nibbled from the bowl, and reached down with one hand and picked it up. It was the runt, and already it was her favorite, maybe because it reminded her of Mozart. She called it Sable, though I think it is more the color of mink. She picked it up to pet it and it scratched her so savagely she dropped it and cried out—not in anger—but in surprise, pain and dismay.

After that we never tried to touch one of the kittens. We were never able to touch their mother, either, and when they were weaned she left their company and our porch. She rarely turned up again, even at mess call. We still see her occasionally in our backyard, back at her wild pursuits, hunting. She seems usually to be stalking something on the ground. We hope it is gophers.

It was soon after we first began putting out food that the survivors of Mona's previous litters began showing up at mealtime. It has become a part of our daily regimen. Whoever gets up first puts the coffee on and opens the front door to see what the count is. Sometimes, as I say, there is no one there; sometimes a dozen. We can't figure out the pattern. We simply feed them, and they accept it.

One morning a year or so ago when one of Mona's Siamese offspring was skulking around in the yard near the fountain, I opened a can of white meat tuna and set it out on the patio. I sat on the back steps, waiting. The cat circled the can, keeping an eye on me, then crept up to it, took a bite and ran. Then it came back. Each time it stole a morsel and bolted, I moved the can closer to the steps.

It took two cans of tuna. Finally I moved the second one into the house, on the kitchen floor. I had the idea that once the cat came indoors and found out how comfortable it was, it would become tame in no time. It came cautiously inside, crept up to the can, and began to nibble. I slipped behind it and quietly shut the door.

The cat went absolutely mad. It dashed for the door, too late; streaked into the living room, raced for the windows, leaped into the glass, hit the carpet running; jumped up on a folded drapery and ripped up to the ceiling; fell; ran to the front door; ran to the back door; leaped into the window again, crashed; crouched, emitted an anguished growl, and looked frantically about, breathing hard.

I was breathing hard too. I was frightened. I wasn't sure I could protect myself if it turned on me.

Quieting my own panic, I slid one of the windows wide open. The next time the cat leaped it went through the window and landed on the patio.

I knew then what wild cat meant.

Until that moment, after more than thirty years on Mt. Washington, I had thought that I was finally beginning to understand cats. Suddenly I felt more mystified than ever.

But that cat hadn't given me my last lesson in the nature of wild cats.

Strangely, though almost every urban neighborhood has them, and there are probably tens of millions in the country, little has been written about feral cats. I have been enlightened if not greatly encouraged, however, by the advice I have received from others. Most of it cautions that it is very difficult to tame a wild cat, if not impossible.

"The feral house cat is the greatest humane problem we have," wrote Katherine Bryant, proprietor of the nonprofit Desert Animal Shelter (which, despite its name, is in the heart of the city). Of our own cats she said, "They are indeed wild animals, and it would take months if ever to turn them into amenable pets. . . ."

A few said they had done it, but it took great patience—more patience, some implied, than I had—and even after a year or two, the housebroken cats remained skittish, suspicious and unpredictable. (It had been my experience that most cats were like that, tame or not.)

But some of the most protective cat people came to our support:

"Many times before," wrote a woman named Myrna Pollock, "I have been prompted by indignation to write you, spurred by your many and sundry insensitive comments about cats. Now I'm glad I never had the time, for you seem to have undergone some minor mellowing in this area. At least your heart appears to be in the right place— to catch and immobilize the kitten factory is indeed a step in the right direction. . . ."

No one had a fool-proof solution to the problem of urban wild cats, but let me summarize, from various bits of advice, the procedure generally recommended.

If you are visited by a wild cat and kittens, put out a dish of food for them every morning and evening, just outside an open door. Don't go near the cats. In time, if you can, catch the mother cat in a cat trap, which you may buy, rent or borrow.

Take her immediately to a veterinarian, clinic or pound, and have her done away with or spayed. If you have her spayed, bring her home and turn her loose. In time follow the same procedure for the kittens, having them neutered or put away. Never, during this period, try to pick up a cat, though gradually you may be able to approach and even touch one.

The main dimension in this scheme is patience, and its ally, time. You need them both, plus a lot of cat food.

What is the best you can hope for? Myrna Pollock sounded experienced and realistic:

"Alas, you can't tame the mama. If you did, it would be a miracle. Getting her spayed, then returning her to her haunts, is all you can do. Yes, there are many vets around who know how to handle dangerous cats as long as they're safely caged. With infinite patience, the kittens can probably be tamed in time, though they will always be on the skittish side, particularly around strangers. . . ."

So what were Denny and I to do?

We decided to go on feeding Mona and her remaining kittens and the cousins and the uncles and the aunts. We would catch the adults as we could, and have them neutered and returned to their haunts, or, if we so decided in our wisdom, have them put away. It would be a long-term project, trying and expensive.

We hoped we might yet tame the kittens, though we knew it was against the odds. We didn't need four kittens, but if we were to keep only one, which one would it be? And what about the other three? Could we have them put away?

I may have mellowed, but I was not yet Solomon.

We were assisted in our project, or perhaps I should say led in it, by a young woman named Lorna, of the Desert Animal Shelter. She came by early one morning, after we had phoned for help, and tried to catch Mona. She brought her own trap, and we stood quietly in the living room, with the front door open, out of sight but listening.

The trap was simply a steel-wire box with a raised door. A dish of food is placed inside near a foot lever, and when the cat steps on the lever the door falls. We heard the door fall. Lorna tiptoed outside. She had caught a kitten. She freed the kitten and set the trap again. This time Mona went in and ate the food but avoided the lever. Lorna went home, promising to try again.

That was the closest we have ever come to trapping Mona.

One morning two weeks later, when the kittens were about three months old, Denny opened the door to make the morning count and saw that the trap was on the porch, set, and that Lorna was sitting in front of the house in her car again, watching.

That turned out to be an exciting morning. Lorna caught Harlequin, the tortoise-shell type with the face divided straight down the nose, black and buff, like a clown's.

When Lorna catches a cat she then throws a cloth over the trap, to calm the prisoner, and drives it to the animal hospital to be spayed, castrated or killed, as we instruct her. (Various euphemisms are used for the word killed among humane people, and I prefer them myself, but killed is what they mean, and I ought to make that clear at least once.)

Quin turned out to be a female, and I told Lorna to have her spayed and bring her home—so to speak. I like her.

After Harlequin had recovered from this adventure, Lorna brought her home and turned her loose. I thought she would put some distance between herself and our front porch, considering her experience, but she soon rejoined the gang.

Encouraged by that success, we asked Lorna to try again. "Lorna's here," Denny said, when she came in a day or two later with the paper.

In a few minutes I heard a thwack and a thrashing sound and realized that something was in the trap. Lorna knocked at the door.

"I caught the black one," she said.

"That monster?" I had committed myself to catching and neutering all our wild ones, returning them to their haunts and feeding them as long as they came around. But the black one was the one I least expected to see in Lorna's trap. He was the rarest of our visitors, evidently having other well-established sources of provender, and when he showed up, like the menace in a western, all in black, the others scattered.

"He's probably the kittens' father," Lorna said.

"Yes," I said, knowing he'd have to be taken care of. The question was, did I want him? Or was Lorna to leave it to her employer for whatever she thought an appropriate disposition? They could place him in a home, which seemed unlikely, or they could have him euphemized.

I didn't know what the black cat's name was, or even that he had one. It was my descriptions of his kind of cat that had given me an unfair reputation as a cat hater. He was stealthy, lustful, greedy and irresponsible. I knew these were instinctive traits, and he couldn't help having them, but I didn't like him anyway.

"Does that brute have a name?" I asked Denny. She was better acquainted with the nomenclature of the tribe than I was.

"Sure," she said. "That's Big Max."

"Oh well, bring him back," I told Lorna.

Do you see the problem? Once you know their names, it's harder to have them put to sleep. Besides, if I deserved a chance to rehabilitate my image, why didn't he?

Lorna transferred him to a cage in her car and set the trap again. I went back to my paper, feeling like an emperor who was casually dispensing destinies. Today I happened to be benign.

In a while there was another commotion.

Lorna had caught Harlequin's sibling, the other mottled tabby. She too was a female.

Lorna took them away. In a day or two she would bring them back, and they would be restored to the street, not knowing and therefore not caring that their sex life was over.

Lorna works for Katherine Bryant, proprietor of the Desert Shelter, and after Lorna returned the first cat, spayed, I received a letter from Mrs. Bryant with an accounting:

"I pay Lorna $7 for each trip, and she has been there four times. That makes $28. I pay her $7 for each cat successfully trapped, which brings the total to $35. In addition, we get a rate from our veterinarian of $20 for spaying cats who aren't pregnant and $25 for pregnant ones. Yours was not pregnant, and that brings the total to $55. Neutering males costs only $15, as it involves a simpler operation."

So the project had cost only $55 so far. But with at least nine cats to go, if none dropped out, and including the two that went into the system that morning, we could see that the enterprise was not going to be cheap.

But already there had been rewards. We received the Desert Shelter's newsletter with its bill, and in it I found this reference to me:

"As some of you noticed, Lorna was recently mentioned in the column of a very prominent local journalist, who honestly wants to do right by his wild cat population. . . ."

That was the first good notice I had ever had in the cat press of America.

36

I may have given the impression that Fleetwood Pugsley was young all his life, and always a clown.

He did grow up, and without putting too sentimental a stamp on it, we grew old together.

Unfortunately, when one has been a comic in his youth, he is always remembered as a comic, and in his maturity, when he retires from slapstick, he doesn't get as much attention.

I believe I have said that Pugsley didn't quite "work out." Actually, *I* was the one who didn't quite work out.

As much as I enjoy our home and our house in Baja and our animals, exasperating though they are at times, I have always been a solitary worker, able to spend long hours in my own company. When I am not reading or at work in my study, I am engaged in the merry-go-round of the city.

I have not been a really good dog man.

I'm afraid Pugsley spent most of his life confined to our yard, and while it is a big yard, perhaps a quarter of an acre inside the fence, and full of ups and downs and shrubbery and shady hiding places (most city dogs would be happy to have it) he would have been happier running free.

Over the years I have seen the neighborhood dogs run up and down our street, dozens of them, sometimes the same ones year after year. Pugsley saw them too. He watched wistfully through the chain-link fence—if a dog can have an emotion as delicate as wistfulness. He no longer even barked at them. He knew them. I suppose he envied them.

Then what was the point of Pugsley and me? Would he have been happier if I'd left him at the kennel where I found him and he'd been bought by someone who would have got his ears glued right and kept him groomed according to the book, and walked him every day, and taught him to heel?

Wouldn't he have been happier if he'd been owned by someone who wouldn't have let Tinker Belle talk them into making a eunuch of him?

I don't know.

Would I have been better off?

No.

We had some good times, and not just when I was laughing at him, either.

We were happiest together when we went down to the house in Baja. Our house is isolated on a plateau above the Santo Tomas Bay. It is wonderful terrain for an Airedale—miles of rugged running room with not a fence in sight, teeming with reptiles and small mammals. How the scents and possibilities of that landscape must have stirred his senses!

I let him run.

You must understand that this is not the sort of beach colony we are familiar with in the United States, with cottages crammed together and streets and sidewalks and picket fences and telephone poles and fire plugs. From our house only two or three others are in sight, and we might as well be at the end of the world, except for the tiny fishing port, a ramshackle scatter of shacks and trailers at the end of the point. We can go days without speaking to anyone or even seeing anyone except fishermen passing by in their pickups over the dirt road that is the only link between the port and Gomez's store a mile the other way.

Between our house and the point a pebbly crescent beach lies at the foot of the cliff. A steep dirt road goes down to the beach from the plateau, and the cove at the bottom is a favorite camping spot for people who dare to risk the descent in their cars.

Pugsley could be counted on to welcome every visitor, and I didn't try to stop him. Sometimes he would be challenged by a dog the visitors had brought, but he never got into a fight, and he made friends with everyone, including hostile dogs, and especially women and children.

Some readers may remember one or two of these small encounters from *God and Mr. Gomez*, the story of our Mexican adventure. It is hard now to picture that house and that landscape without Pugsley.

Little things. One morning he went down to the beach to call on a family that had come in during the night. I knew he must be disrupting their breakfast, if they were trying to eat outdoors, and decided I'd better fetch him home.

They were Americans. They had chairs out around a fire and were cooking breakfast. Pugs was getting acquainted. I put his leash on him and two small girls and a boy came up to us looking disappointed.

"Is that your dog?" one said.

"Yes. He's mine."

"What kind is he?"

"He's a watchdog."

"He sure is friendly for a watchdog."

"That's his way," I said. "He likes to get acquainted with people so he knows whether he ought to bark at them or not."

That evening, about dinnertime, I missed him again. Again I got the leash and walked down to the beach. He was romping with a girl in a bikini. She had just made an enormous hamburger and had broken off a bite which she held out to Pugs.

"Does he like hamburger?" she asked.

"I suppose so," I said. "He's never turned down anything yet."

He made a feint at the bite she was holding out to him, then struck for the other hand and snatched the entire hamburger.

"With tomato and onions," the girl said.

One Sunday when there were several parties visiting in the area, he ran off just when we were getting ready to leave for home. We finished loading the car and locked up and drove out looking for him. I knew he would have joined up with some family. We drove all the way to the port and finally found him on the way back. He was with a man and a woman with three children and a dog. Everyone seemed to know everyone.

I called him: "Here Pugs, here boy!"

He looked at me as if trying to remember who I was.

"What's his name?" asked one of the children.

"Pugsley," I said. "Fleetwood Pugsley."

"Well," the man said, "we call him Jake."

That was how quickly and unconditionally people took him in. Right away they gave him a name.

He didn't really have much to do with another memorable incident; but I will never forget it because of what he surely would have done, if I hadn't stopped him just in time.

The landscape looked deserted one morning when we went down the road in the gully to the beach, and I was surprised to see a Volkswagen at the bottom in the cove, and a light camp set out around a beach blanket. I heard shrill cries and out in the surf I saw figures bobbing, wet blond hair and fair skin flashing in the sun. They looked like two girls and a boy, though I wasn't sure.

I walked on, beyond the pebbles, to the wide sandy beach that stretches for half a mile below the cliffs. Pugsley ran ahead, splashing in the surf, chasing seagulls, nosing tidepools. Suddenly he spied something far ahead and rollicked off. I caught up to find him lavishing briny kisses on two small children. They were trying to hug him. Their parents stood nearby, grinning uncertainly. They had come down from a camper at the top of the cliff.

"He loves children," I assured them unnecessarily.

I tugged him away and we started back. He was lagging behind, sporting in the surf, when I neared the little camp. The swimmers were back. The three of them were stretched out on the blanket face down. The girls appeared to be wearing nothing but pale pink bikini bottoms. They looked nubile and vulnerable. Suddenly I realized that they weren't wearing bikini bottoms. They weren't wearing anything.

I would just walk by. The surf would cover the sound of my steps on the pebbles. They'd never know I had seen them. Suddenly I remembered the Airedale. I turned. He was galloping toward me, two seconds away, his muzzle dripping seaweed. There was no doubt what he would do when he saw the people on the blanket. He would be on them in an instant, planting icy kisses on whatever targets providence provided.

I grabbed him by the collar just as he reached my side and spied the luscious prizes on the blanket. I tugged him away and we struggled silently around the camp and up the road. They had never been aware of our presence.

It was just one more joy I had deprived him of. But for once it hurt me more than it did him.

I have never known a gentler dog. Even Shaggy had her snappish moments. Pugs never snapped, never snarled. None of the abuses thought up by a relay team of five grandchildren ever cracked his patience. Not that he was stupid or insensitive. He was simply good.

Incredibly, he didn't even harass the cats, though how he managed to curb his terrier instincts in their behalf I can't imagine.

The gas-meter reader and the pool man and others who had to open the gate and come into the yard were intimidated at first, when they looked over the fence and saw an Airedale; but one experience with him and they were never nervous again.

Pugs slowed down after he passed the decade mark, but it was not especially noticeable until he was twelve or thirteen years old. Then he seemed to be deteriorating. His eye was not as sharp; his carriage not as jaunty; his gait not as lithe and graceful. His appetite fell off. He didn't enjoy barking. He spent hours in his doghouse. Sometimes he cried out.

I took him to Dr. Morehouse. "Jack," he said, "he's old."

"Nothing I should be doing for him?"

He shook his head.

"They don't live forever," he said.

He lived quite a long time, growing less and less agile, less and less alert and active.

I made up my mind. Unless he was obviously suffering, I was not going to have him put down. Ending it before he became a complete invalid was the easy way, for us, perhaps, and perhaps for him. It had been the only way with Gus and maybe the best way with the others.

But Pugsley would go the route, just as I probably would, civilized morality being what it is.

He didn't come out of his house one evening when I went out with his bowl.

He had gone the route.

EPILOGUE

Our yard will never be quite the same without Fleetwood Pugsley. It is like a happy little kingdom whose king is dead, and there is no successor.

I have it in my mind that there will be none. Another Pugsley, I'm afraid, would be too much for my old age.

We still have Fluff, the would-be Yorkie. She is alone now, with George's cats, though they are no longer just George's cats—they are ours, too; and they belong to no one. They are still wild.

We have not been able to catch and neuter them all, and we suspect that one of the kittens is pregnant. Obviously, it is never to end.

Denny is pleased that the kitten she liked best, Sable, seems to have made our porch her home. She is the one regular in the bunch. Even she, though, will not yet allow herself to be touched.

We are trying to be patient. I want that little cat to trust me, as true proof of my rehabilitation.

The red setter that came into the house that rainy night years ago is still a visitor. He has the luck of the Irish, surely, to have survived the hazards of the streets so long. I have been tempted to take him in; he seems to be eating half the cat food anyway. But I know he would never stay. He's a rover.

The Daltons have moved away from the hill. He retired from the university and they meant to live in Tahiti, but they stayed in Papeete only two weeks. It rained without cease, and Mrs. Dalton was disenchanted.

Now they live in an apartment in Pasadena, only a few miles away, and we see them often, but I miss having Dalton on the hill. Nobody is watching birds and wild animals for me on his side of the canyon.

I wonder whether the new owners of their house set out sandwiches for the raccoons at night, the way Dalton did; or did he just make that story up?

Pooh-Bah, the cockatiel, is still with us. He is noisy enough, but as far as I can make out he still doesn't say anything (in English) but "Big deal!" which makes me uneasy.

Pitti-Sing, the canary, was short-lived, and has been succeeded by another canary and a parakeet. I am beginning to feel like a bird in a gilded cage myself.

I have never seen another grackle, and if they are as noisy and mean as I have heard, I am in no hurry to see one.

There is an Airedale on the hill. I suspect it is

the one that Denny caught that day thinking it was Pugs. I see him sometimes when I'm coming home, or leaving. He may be a block away—trotting, or just standing there, and looking so familiar that I sometimes touch the brake before I realize that it can't be Pugs.

And silently I laugh. Usually when I think of Pugs I laugh.